WINNING COMPLEX
ENTERPRISE SALES

WINNING COMPLEX ENTERPRISE SALES

A TRUE STORY OF THE BEST CAMPAIGN EVER...
FOR SALES TEAMS, CIVIC AND POLITICAL
LEADERS...CONSENSUS GENERATION AT ITS BEST

Bud Suse

Copyright © 2016 Bud Suse
All rights reserved. No part of this publication may be reproduced, stored in a retrieval system, or transmitted, in any form or by any means, electronic, mechanical, photocopying, recording, or otherwise, without the written prior permission of the author.
ISBN: 1523299215
ISBN 13: 9781523299218
Library of Congress Control Number: 2016901023
CreateSpace Independent Publishing Platform
North Charleston, South Carolina

Additional Books by Bud Suse

Closing the Whales

Winning Complex

Enterprise Sales

A True Story of the Best Campaign Ever...

For Sales Teams. Community and Political Leaders...

Consensus Generation at its Best

DEDICATION

This book is dedicated to my wonderful family who has enriched my days beyond measure.

Further, it is dedicated to all salespeople who pursue complex enterprise campaigns...and the book is dedicated to the application and systems engineers, without whose support, few complex enterprise campaigns would ever be won.

ACKNOWLEDGEMENTS

This book is an instruction book on the interesting subject of complex Enterprise sales campaign management. It is also a primer for broad-based consensus generation. The audiences for which it is intended, of course, are sales people, account managers, sales teams, local or national government entities, citizens groups, school boards, hospital administrators, etc. In other words, the audience is any person or organization that hopes to launch and prevail in a serious campaign via consensus generation.

As a model for instruction on the subject, I know of no more fascinating and instructive story than the campaign for the Denver International Airport that began in 1978 and culminated 17 years later in 1995, and therefore, I acknowledge and applaud Robert

L. "Bob" Albin, who generated the idea and championed the campaign for 17 years as an unpaid citizen volunteer, and I acknowledge and applaud the Denver Metro Chamber of Commerce Board of Directors of that period, which sponsored the campaign and contributed so significantly to the campaign.

Further, I thank and acknowledge Doak Jacoway and Ned Minor, two past chairmen of the Denver Metro Chamber of Commerce Board of Directors and two reliable historians of the campaign, for introducing the story of the campaign to me and for their assistance with this book.

Finally, I acknowledge and appreciate the work of Fred Brown, the acclaimed Denver Post journalist whose book, <u>The Persistence of Vision</u>, <u>The Denver Metro Chamber of Commerce</u>, captured the inspirational story of Denver and the Region's history, particularly, the story of the bold measure taken by the Board of Trade, the predecessor to the Denver Metro Chamber of Commerce, in 1870 to insure the Region's connection to the outside world via a rail spur line connecting Denver to the first trans-continental railway in Cheyenne, Wyoming. Fred Brown's detail-rich account of the campaign for the New Denver Airport, now known as DIA, was not only an intriguing story. It was extremely helpful in the development of this book, and again my thanks.

The Cardinal Sin of Complex Enterprise Campaigns is Coming in a Close Second

Anonymous

TABLE OF CONTENTS

FORWARD

When I was 16, I got one of my first summer jobs working for a satellite company. It wasn't the kind of satellites we're used to talking about today; these satellites were the big ones out in the back yard that brought cable television programming into your home if you lived too far out in the country to get cable.

The sales process went something like this: I would drive around in my car looking for homes that didn't have cable (bet you didn't know that you could know that just by looking at the power poles around the neighborhood!). When I would find an area deprived of quality television programming, I would get my clipboard out and go door-to-door, taking a survey to see who would want cable if it suddenly became available on their street.

Nine times out of 10, my prospects would answer with an enthusiastic *Yes!* Next question, "Would you like to set an appointment for tomorrow at this same time to meet with a cable TV representative?" Another *Yes.* The next day at the appointed time, their cable TV representative (that would be me) would arrive to discuss with them the affordable satellite that could magically bring cable television programming into their living room. For just one dollar down and a modest payment plan over the next 36 months, I'd sign them up to have a large C-ban satellite installed in their back yard that would allow them the opportunity to channel surf just like the city slickers in town who got cable.

Thirty-something years later, I look back on that and think about how easy it was: *They got cable TV. I'd make a commission.* Today I run two international companies that depend on sales to drive revenue and growth. Oh, how I wish our sales process and sales cycle were as simple and short as my days of selling satellites.

On a cold winter day about two years ago, I was sitting in my chair in the living room, surfing the Internet looking for books on how to sell large deals more easily. I came across a little gem of a book by Bud Suse entitled *Closing the Whales: The Anatomy of Major*

Deals – A Proven Process for Complex, High Tech Sales Campaigns. Based on its reviews on Amazon, it seemed like the exact book I was looking for. The problem was that Amazon didn't have it any more. It was out of print. The only copies for sale by the affiliates were either badly used or very expensive. So, I did a quick Internet search for Bud Suse and found a website with his contact info.

I shot off an email to Bud, asking if I could buy a book directly from him. Much to my amazement, a couple of days later I got a most unexpected email back from him. He said he'd be glad to send me a book for free and would even be open to a phone call– if I was interested. I immediately reached out to him and spent a wonderful half hour hearing his story and sharing mine. He'd retired from IBM years earlier and had long since quit promoting his book. Before long, Bud and I had devised a plan for him to take a break from his boring, golf-every-day retirement in southern California to come conduct a two-day sales training session with our team in Nashville, Tennessee.

Bud Suse knows how to run large complex sales cycles. His unassuming presence and gentle personality wonderfully hide one of the most amazingly gifted sales professionals I have ever met. His ability to see straight through the muck and mire of most complex sales processes is superhuman. Our team was blown away, and it set our course on a much higher plane. Within a few months of implementing his methods and strategies, we were awarded over $1M in new contracts. To this day, we quote Bud in our sales meetings.

When Bud asked me to review his manuscript for this new book, I was honored and excited. As you will soon find out for yourself in the pages of this book, Bud's decades of successful experience running large, long-cycle, complex, technical sales campaigns will shine light into the dark corners of getting deals closed. Most of all, you'll learn how to make sure that if you're going to lose, you lose early. Bud taught us that most sales people know what a "yes" sounds like from a prospect; the reality, though, is that very few know what a "no" sounds like.

In the pages of this book, you will learn how to pay attention to process and chart your progress through a sales campaign so that you don't waste time on deals that go nowhere. *Winning Complex Enterprise Sales* should be required reading for all sales managers and team leaders who engage in large enterprise sales campaigns. It is simple, straightforward, honest, and reasonable. What it definitely is NOT is gimmicky. If you're looking for the next trendy way to sell, this isn't it. But if you're looking for a time-honored, proven way to engage large enterprise customers in a complex sales process, you've found the Holy Grail.

Jason Duncan

Gallatin, Tennessee, 2016

President and CEO, Future Vision Energy

Chairman, Teslights

PREFACE

This is a "How To" book, so I assume that anyone motivated to read it is in search of a deeper understanding of, in this case, how to win complex Enterprise campaigns. So I should tell you up front what you can expect to find in the book as well as what you will not find, starting with the latter.

This is not a book of sales gimmicks or sales techniques. It is not a book of guarantees or shortcuts. You won't find anything here about how to annihilate your toughest competitor.

What you will find in this book, instead, is an exemplary story of a magnificent achievement resulting from a massive campaign void of misrepresentation, an absence of spin or anything close to shady underhanded business ethics. Instead, you will witness a campaign, steadfastly focused on a higher purpose, guided by a set of principles embracing the most honorable campaign ethics for the greater good of a city and a region.

The private sector, the Denver Metro Chamber of Commerce, initiated the campaign for the New Denver Airport, which is the central story in this book, exemplifying best practices in complex campaign management. But once launched, the support and positive contribution of key political figures cannot be overstated. For example, Denver Mayor, Federico Pena, was a tireless campaigner in the city and county of Denver for the New Denver Airport. The legendary account of Governor Roy Romer's daily oatmeal breakfasts…no sugar…no milk in nearly every restaurant in Adams County that serves breakfast, gave him a chance to meet people, answer questions and promote the campaign.

I said this campaign embraced the highest business ethics in the creation of this book in the Acknowledgement. Appreciation was given to four men. Here is a quick introduction to these gentlemen.

Ned Minor is a successful attorney, located in Denver, and is a former Chairman of the Denver Metro Chamber of Commerce

Board of Directors and knows the history of the campaign for the New Denver Airport as well as anyone. Ned has spent his professional life helping people who are considering selling their business. As an attorney focused on the subject, His book, <u>Deciding to Sell Your Business</u> is an example of exemplary high standards in the service for people who are about to enter unknown territory.

Doak Jacoway, too, is a former Chairman of the Denver Metro Chamber of Commerce Board of Directors. Jacoway founded and manages his company, Jacoway Financial Corporation, located in Denver.

Much later in this book, I make the case that the ability to identify, initiate and manage multiple major campaigns concurrently is the defining difference between true professionals, who enjoy extended accomplishments over time, versus those who manage campaigns on a serial, one-at-a time basis.

Jacoway's talent for managing multiple projects concurrently is well-documented. Here are a few examples:

From a casual but pivotal conversation with the Denver Broncos owner, Pat Bowlen, who quietly mentioned to Jacoway that he needed a new stadium, Jacoway recognized the serious-ness of the comment and aggressively initiated the new Denver Broncos Stadium campaign and proactively supported the drive resulting in the Broncos's new home...now known as Sports Authority Field at Mile High.

During Doak Jacoway's term as Chamber Chairman, one of his priorities was transportation, which included the continued expan-sion of light rail for reinvigorating Downtown Denver. Denver's first light rail line, opened for business on October 7, 1994 with 5.3 miles of line. In the year 2000, expansion began. Today Denver's light rail system serves 47 miles of track over 6 lines.

During Doak Jacoway's tenure as the Board Chairman, as mentioned, transportation was a top priority. In terms of accom-plishments, the expanded light rail system and the highway ex-pansion of I-25, known as the Transportation Project, T-REX, were major achievements for the Denver Metro region.

However, while in that job, his greatest accomplishment some would argue was as Chairman of the Committee for implement-ing the findings of a 50 year strategic plan for the development of Denver's business future. Those findings added focus to 2 new industries that Denver should develop – space science and bio – science, as natural adjuncts to its' existing business drivers of agriculture, government, tourism, finance, manufacturing and distribution.

So as you can see, Doak Jacoway has a decades-long track record of leadership in community services for Denver, and he, too, is at the top of a list of reliable historians who can cite the factual account of the campaign for the New Denver Airport.

Appreciating the launching and management of the airport campaign, Doak Jacoway initiated the idea of publishing a book about the campaign for the New Denver Airport. The book's author, cited in the Acknowledgement, is Fred Brown, the highly acclaimed, well-known and respected journalist located in Denver. He is the retired Capitol Bureau Chief for the Denver Post.

Earlier, I stated what this book is not about. I would add to that statement saying that it is not an effort to give an in-depth account of the complexities of the campaign for the New Airport. Fred Brown has already accomplished that mission, and I strongly recommend his book. The book is fascinating history.

Brown is a champion for journalism ethics and has been throughout his illustrious career. In fact, at Denver University's Journalism School, Brown teaches a required course in journalism ethics. Here, is peer praise for Fred Brown that honors his commitment for doing things right in journalism.

CHICAGO – "The Society of Professional Journalists is pleased to honor Fred Brown with the Wells Memorial Key, the Society's highest honor.

The Wells Memorial Key is given to a member for outstanding service to the Society during the preceding year or over a period of years. Here are a couple of comments from the Society:

"Fred Brown demonstrates how to use our SPJ Code of Ethics, not as a club, but as a tool to reason with other journalists and members of the public on thorny issues," wrote Irwin Gratz, SPJ past president, in his nomination.

"As an officer, board member and ethics committee chair, he championed professionalism at every turn, led at every key occasion and quietly reminded everyone who would listen of the importance of ethics," wrote Paul McMasters, SPJ past president, in his nomination.

Brown was nominated by 12 past presidents of the Society. He was the national president of SPJ in 1997-98, having stepped in when the president-elect left the position. He also has been the Region 9 director, president of the Colorado Pro chapter and is currently on the board of the Sigma Delta Chi Foundation.

More recognition for Fred Brown: He has received the Journalist of the Year and the Board of Directors awards from the Colorado Pro chapter. He has won the Sigma Delta Chi national award for editorial writing, was inducted into the Denver Press Club Hall of Fame in 2003, and was the 2001 Colorado Newspaperperson of the Year.

Finally, I acknowledged Bob Albin, who is also a past Chairman of the Denver Metro Chamber of Commerce Board of Directors. I thank him for his permission to use the story to be told, his role in the campaign for the New Denver Airport and for reviewing the manuscript of this book

Bob Albin's professional resume is impressive: He was a Co-Founder & President of American Salesmasters and is a retired Chief Operating Officer of Western Union North America.

When I spoke to Albin asking his blessings for my telling the story of the New Denver Airport campaign as a model of campaign management best practices, the purpose of the book, he agreed that the campaign met the elements of complex campaign management. He had no objections to my telling the story on two conditions: He said that his role should not be embellished, because, as he said, "Lots of people besides me contributed to the campaign significantly." He emphasized, "I should not be portrayed as the "Shining Knight" leading every charge nor should I be portrayed as the one making every decision or directing every action. Nothing could be further from the truth. This was a massive campaign and there were lots of leadership from lots of people."

Interesting author's note... At the time this is being written, our country is in the middle of a national election year. Day in and day out the candidates, in booming voices proclaim their utterly amazing ability to lead us to the Promised Land. In contrasting style and tone, given the opportunity to applaud himself, Bob Albin, instead, took the opportunity to praise a number of other people, especially Mayor Federico Pena for his leadership and decisive actions during the campaign. Too, Albin voiced his respect and admiration for Governor Roy Romer's sponsorship and tireless leadership. Albin was emphatic about the fact that both men put their political interests aside for the greater good of Denver and the Region. In the case of Mayor Pena, the Mayor was acutely aware that he would not be in office by the time the airport would become a reality. In fact, Pena later served as Secretary of Transportation and Secretary of Energy during the Bill Clinton presidency.

To paraphrase Albin's opinion of Mayor Pena and Governor Romer, "From their leadership actions and dedication to the campaign, those two men showed their true colors, honorable men who would spend their time, energy and personal capital for a mission bigger than themselves."

Albin explained that the campaign was massively complex and moved forward on many fronts, far too many for any one person to lead every front.

Praising the mayor and governor's contributions, along with several others he again asked, "Don't embellish my role in the book"

Second, Albin said he had no objections for my including the story in my book so long as the telling of the story was completely factual.

So, in honoring his requirement that the following account of the campaign be completely factual, that has been accomplished. And in honoring his requirement to avoid embellishing his role in the campaign and to tone it down, that, too, has been attempted. Of course, during the campaign, Mayor Pena conducted many news conferences, and who was often standing at his side lending his credibility and wholehearted support? You guessed it...Bob Albin. So as to the role he played in the campaign, you decide.

Author's note: Reviewing the manuscript of this book, two historians of the campaign for the New Denver Airport and Albin's role in it, Ned Minor and Doak Jacoway, have both expressed to me, categorically, that Bob Albin's role in the campaign in this book has not been embellished, and the facts, as presented, are one hundred percent true.

The reason I have included such detail about the four men acknowledged is not to promote them or heap unbiased or unsolicited praise. None of these four accomplished men neither want nor need it. I am acknowledging them with necessary detail because of the conservative, ageless ethical requirement for reporting: If you are going to tell an important story, intelligent people will insist on hard proof, like who are your multiple sources and are they reliably objective and legitimate? I suggest that these four men know the intimate details of the campaign for the New Denver Airport better than almost anyone, and their credentials are impeccable. Further, prior to the publishing of this book, each reviewed the content of the manuscript for barebones accuracy and good taste...put another way, the campaign story and the participant's roles included are completely factual and void of excessive embellishment

INTRODUCTION

What is the difference between a "Complex Sale" and an "Enterprise Sale?" The answer is: Nothing I'm suggesting that you not get too hung up on what is a "Complex" campaign versus an "Enterprise" campaign. Fundamentally, as I indicated, they are the same.

Wikipedia offers an extended definition. Here is the short version.

"Complex <u>sales</u>, also known as Enterprise sales, can refer to a method of trading, sometimes used, by organizations when procuring large contracts for goods and/or services where the customer takes control of the selling process by issuing a <u>Request for Proposal</u> (RFP) and requiring a <u>proposal</u> response from previously identified or interested suppliers. Complex sales involve long sales cycles with multiple decision makers. Multiple stakeholders and stakeholder groups contribute to every complex sale."

Since we now have a definition of Complex or Enterprise sales from Wikipedia, you might think...enough is enough, but for our purposes, which is what counts...The real definition of an Enterprise deal hinges on the management style of the prospect. Simply put, does the prospect have several voters and influencers involved in significant buying decisions or not? In other words, is the prospect's decision-making process a consensus management style or a top-down process?

The purpose of this book is how to win large, complex sales opportunities. It is not about chasing the mega deal with multiple silos involved in the voting process. Instead it is geared to what sales managers and account managers consider very significant opportunities in a prospect environment more complex than that of a single buyer.

The size of the opportunity is the first consideration for defining an Enterprise sale. It needs to meet your definition of "Big."

The second consideration that defines an Enterprise opportunity is about the number of people involved... the various lower level managers, C-Level Executives, users, departments, etc. that are involved in the decision for implementation. The opportunity needs to meet your definition of complexity...not simple.

Therefore, the simple definition of an Enterprise deal is this. If it is quite large...big, and if it is complex because more than one person is involved in the decision...especially, if there are several people involved in the decision, the opportunity is an Enterprise deal.

For our purposes of closing larger opportunities and gaining higher productivity as a result, that is enough of a definition for me. I suggest it is for you, too.

My Personal Enterprise Selling Experience

As I mentioned in the introduction, most of my career has been spent in the technology world as a sales manager, account manager and later as an Enterprise campaign sales consultant. During those years I either conducted, helped conduct or at close range, as the second level sales manager, observed the orchestration of dozens of successful Enterprise sales. I have reconstructed enough Enterprise deals by the specific events that were orchestrated in those deals, from first hellos to solution delivery, to be completely confident that what you will learn from the following pages will help you move from simpler, smaller but quick transactions to bigger and more rewarding Enterprise deals.

From a sales training perspective, having spent 12 years with IBM, I have been trained thoroughly on consultative selling. Additionally, my training experience includes a number of the better known commercially available sales training courses.

I point this fact out for one reason. Nearly all the training courses I have had focus on how one person successfully persuades another individual. Enterprise consensus generation, as you will see, is an entirely different subject and requires an additional set of skills.

As an introduction, the focus of this book will be on those applied principles and skills required for success in winning complex Enterprise campaign

CHAPTER 1

THE POWER OF THE VISION
AND THE MASTER MIND

I f you have ever written a book or a significant paper, proposal or letter, you know how much thought you put into the question, "Where should I begin?" And I'm no different.

In my case, I started with a few conclusions: I concluded that I don't now nor have I ever had an original idea. It is safe to say that every idea I embrace came from someone else.

I concluded that if this book is well received, regardless of the number who read it, it will be because of the helpful insight given to me by the people I acknowledged earlier.

I concluded, too, that there are certain principles in life pertaining to successfully realizing a vision that are timeless, just as valid today as they were one hundred years ago.

Finally, I concluded that you, the reader, didn't acquire this book on a whim. You acquired it for a reason: you saw something about the book that might help you in an Enterprise opportunity you are pursuing or about to pursue, and you have every intention of winning

That, then, is my conclusion and premise. So the purpose of this book is to give you the foundation for managing a complex Enterprise sales campaign. I have wrestled with the question as I mentioned earlier, "Where should I begin?"

I decided that nothing would be more important than passing on to you a philosophy articulated by Napoleon Hill decades ago in his now famous book, Think and Grow Rich. In his book, he offers the wisdom, with which so many of you are intimately familiar, "Whatever the mind can conceive and believe, it can achieve."

I can assure you that that basic truth will be clearly evident in the story to be told later in this book, because the man who launched the most massive and complex Enterprise campaign imaginable, first had a realistic and immensely valuable vision.

And he had an unshakable confidence the vision could become reality. Further, from his social and professional experience, knowing the collective synergistic strength from companionship and collaboration, he formed close alliances, close associations with colleagues, who bought into the vision and who also believed the vision would become a reality. You will see the effectiveness of that practice in the campaign for the New Denver Airport.

What I have just described is Napoleon Hill's 2nd Principle, one that he calls "The Master Mind." In terms of getting started in winning a complex Enterprise sales campaign, the best advice I can give you is to, first, accept the fact that "Whatever the mind can conceive and believe it can achieve" is the real deal. It works. Connected with that is accepting that when you practice the Master Mind principle, today known in sales lingo as, "Intensive Account Planning," you will substantially increase the intellectual quotient (IQ) of tactical and strategic conclusions guiding your campaign. Because of the significance of applying this fundamental principle, here is the essence of Napoleon Hill's 2nd Principle.

Napoleon Hill: On the Master Mind Alliance

- A Master Mind may be developed by a friendly alliance, in a spirit of harmony of purpose, between two or more minds. No two minds ever met without creating, as a result of the contact, another mind which affects all participating in the alliance.

- This principle is analogous to chemistry. For example, the chemical formula H_2O (combining two atoms of hydrogen with one atom of oxygen) changes these two elements to water. One atom of each of these elements will not produce water; moreover, they cannot even be made to associate themselves in harmony.

- Just as combining certain elements changes their nature, the combining of certain minds changes the nature of those minds, producing either a certain degree of a Master Mind or its highly destructive opposite. Very simply, a Master Mind may be defined as the invisible power that results when two or more minds work in perfect harmony toward achieving a common goal.

- The ability to organize people in strategic positions in a spirit of friendliness and harmony was the main source of both the power and the fortune accumulated by the late Andrew Carnegie. Knowing nothing of the technical end of the steel business, Carnegie combined and grouped the key executives of which his Master Mind was composed, so that in his lifetime he built the most successful steel industry the world had known.

- Henry Ford's gigantic success may be traced to the application of this same principle. Ford was extremely self-reliant, but he did not depend upon himself for all the knowledge necessary for the development of his business. Like Carnegie, he surrounded himself with men who supplied knowledge, which he did not, and probably never could, possess. Moreover, he selected men who could, and did, harmonize in group effort. Harmony seems to be one of nature's laws, without which there cannot be any such thing as organized energy. Without harmony at the source of any form of organized energy or power, the units of that energy are thrown into a chaotic state of disorder and the power is rendered neutral or passive

- This same harmony is the nucleus around which the principle of mind chemistry known as a Master Mind develops power. Destroy this harmony, and you destroy the power growing out of the coordinated effort of a group of individual minds.

- Success in life, no matter what your definition of success may be, is very largely a matter of adaptation to the environment in such a manner that there is harmony between the individual and the environment. Harmony is essential; without it, the entire world would be chaos and disorder.

- Harmony creates organization of knowledge by harmonizing facts, truths, and natural laws. It provides order among the stars and planets in the universe, and among the collection of individuals that makes up all great organizations.

- It is not always easy to achieve such harmony. Every human being possesses internal forces that are difficult to harmonize, even when he is placed in a most favorable environment. Think how much more difficult it is to harmonize a group of minds so that they will function as one in an orderly manner.

- A successful leader must be able to direct the Master Mind by using tact, patience, persistence, self-confidence, knowledge, and the ability to adapt himself (in a state of perfect poise and harmony) to quickly changing circumstances without the slightest sign of annoyance.

- Of course, some minds simply will not blend in a spirit of harmony, and cannot be forced to do so. Do not, however, be too quick to charge others in your alliance with all the responsibility for the lack of harmony. The trouble may be with your own mind.

- Remember, also, that a mind, which cannot and will not harmonize with one person or group, may harmonize perfectly with other types of minds. There are many instances where misfits in one job went on to achieve great success in another field. If you are not sure that you understand this law, analyze the record of anyone who has accumulated a great fortune, and you will find that in every case such people have consciously or unconsciously employed the Master Mind principle.

- The acid test of any theory or rule or principle is that it will actually work. The law of the Master Mind has been proven sound because it works. It has been used effectively by leaders throughout the history of business, politics, and philosophy. Many of our greatest advances have been made through the successful use of the Master Mind principle. It will work for you, too, if you let it."

In the modern era, we have only to look at the close alliance of Bill Gates and Paul Allen as they founded Microsoft, later adding Steve Ballmer.

Witness how Steve Jobs and Steve Wozniak, working in Job's parent's garage, founded Apple Computer Company.

Another example is how President Lincoln formed his cabinet.

His cabinet included all of his major rivals for the Republican nomination: William H. Seward, Salmon P. Chase, Simon Cameron and Edward Bates. Later, there would be cabinet changes. These were strong men, and they had differences over ideology, ethics and personality. Many of them objected to the inclusion of each other. Yet they respected Lincoln, listened to his views, expressed their own, and together effected a cabinet synergy that guided the administration through a pivotal period in the Nation's history.

President Lincoln, of course, knew the conflicts among the cabinet would be ongoing. Yet he knew, too, that each could contribute, particularly, in the job of generating wide-based consensus, a united front, for meeting the enormous challenges before the country. Lincoln also suspected, apparently, that he would develop close relationships with at least some of his cabinet, and he did. For example, he and Seward, and a later appointment, Stanton, became very close.

There are countless other examples of close associations that generated exceptional synergy resulting in amazing accomplishments, so combined with a clear vision, this, I believe, is where most winning campaigns start.

Intensive Account Planning

I have always appreciated the philosophy of Napoleon Hill, and I witnessed it and experienced it, specifically, in 1988, when our small startup company closed 28 Enterprise contracts of $1M or more. The following year, we closed an equal number of contracts, but they were much larger, some as much as $25M. What every single campaign had in common was: each campaign began with an Intensive Account Planning Session.

Intensive account planning sessions are vital to the launching of a campaign, and it is equally important to keep having them through the duration of the campaign including implementation, delivery.

You will see in the campaign for The New Denver Airport that dozens on top of dozens of intense planning and collaboration sessions were conducted.

Intensive Account Planning, the Master Mind principle, is team, collaborative planning with a common goal. The value of team, collaborative thinking is no longer a debatable question. Scientifically, we know it produces better results than independent thinking, thinking in a vacuum. Intensive Account Planning Sessions occur in virtually every campaign that requires an account manager and any support person working together as a team throughout the life of the campaign. The quality and intensity of those sessions range from two people in a coffee shop, with the events planned and written on the back of an envelope to structured sessions in a crowded board room, with lots of bodies participating and elaborate account plans devised.

I was first introduced to the concept at IBM in October, 1973. Off to White Plains, New York I went to attend a week's training on a concept called "Intensive Account Planning" for major accounts. Any subject that takes a week to teach to a group of experienced sales managers is too much detail for our purposes in this book. Suffice it to say, on the subject of "Intensive Account Planning for major accounts, there was a great deal of instruction relative to who, what, where, when, how and why. Here is the quick answer to those six questions:

1. Who? Team huddle! Everybody on the account team is required to attend, start to finish. The best sessions include your customer sponsors and mentors.

2. What? Understand the account, the opportunity, everything relative about the account and the opportunity.

3. Where? It took a week for IBM to get through this question, but the short answer is the session should be offsite. Again, no distractions, no part-time attendees, no rathole subjects, no intimidation or ridicule of others. The focus is on structured research with the goal of an action plan complete with calendar commitments and follow-up process.

4. When? At the birth of the idea, continuing soon and often after positive qualifying. Session durations can last as little as a few minutes to as long as three days or more, if necessary.

5. How? Led by the person who generated the idea with rules to be respected. See Napoleon Hill's guidelines above.

6. Why? Enterprise accounts keep a company in business, and eventually require less mundane handholding than small accounts. The big reason is an Enterprise account is where the gold is!

I have participated in a number of Intensive Account Planning sessions involving national major accounts in Western Europe,

Asia, Latin America, Canada and Australia as well as in The United States. I have modified the concept, shortening the normal length of the sessions. Before I close on this subject, here is a short list of lessons learned in the process.

1. A very good session can be conducted in three four-hour sessions. Three-day sessions can be very expensive in time and dollars, and while long sessions can be justified in many cases, getting buy-in from the organizations involved with the team is easier with abbreviated versions.

2. Invite team members in writing, and make assignments abundantly clear with accountability equally clear.

3. A first cousin to the first lesson is that planning can be overdone. Written account plans can be overdone. Five pound, five-ring binders that nobody looks at after the assignment is complete have little value to anyone other than the supply store that sells big binders. I would much prefer a single page of well-conceived action items that each team member fully supports than the giant document that puts everyone to sleep.

4. Either get buy-in from participating organizations, get the homework completed right, get the undivided attention of the participants, get the right level of integrity to the sessions or don't have them. Don't expect good results from half-hearted efforts.

5. Generally your client or customer sponsor will have a vested interest in your success. Include your sponsors and mentors for at least one of the four-hour sessions as part of the team.

6. Stop when you are done, when you and the team have accomplished your mission. If a miracle happens, and you get everything done during the first four-hour session, so much the better, unlikely though it may be.

Keep in mind that this event is like all the other events available to you in your event framework. It is your option. You may choose not to. It is also always a good idea to assume that your competitor has already conducted a thorough "Intensive Account Planning Session," and has a strategy, a strategy that you need to understand and defeat. After all, your objective in competing is to defeat your competitor's strategy.

Significant Points of Review

- Create a vision

- Form close relationships with those who share your vision

- Conduct intensive planning sessions often

CHAPTER 2

THE BIGGEST AND BEST CAMPAIGN EVER...LESSONS LEARNED

A few years ago, after nearly 30 years of sales and sales management and a decade spent in Enterprise sales campaign coaching, I wrote a brief 128 page instruction book on closing whale size deals, Enterprise deals. The book's title...Closing The Whales.

I was never under any illusion that the book would be a high-volume seller. In fact, at the time the manuscript was submitted, the publisher asked me how many books I expected to sell, and my response was, "Maybe a few hundred." But as the months since publishing have turned into years, every week people either find it on Amazon and buy it or check it out from the Kindle Free Library

This book is about you. It is about my mission to bring you the collective experience and wisdom of dozens of account managers and sales managers who were very successful in competing in Enterprise sales campaigns.

My sincere hope is that you will find good value in the following pages, that these pages lift your confidence and strengthen your skill set for the campaigns ahead.

The goal in writing this book, too, is to give you a clear idea of how to launch and succeed in the complex Enterprise selling arena. In so doing, as a picture is worth a thousand words, a true story will be remembered longer than a set of instructions.

The story to be told is, in fact, the instruction, because it clearly illuminates Enterprise Campaign Management best practices. So let's look at what those best practices are and how you can adopt them to your efforts.

At the heart, Enterprise campaign management is the process of gaining consensus among a wide group of stakeholders. Every action and event of the campaign is a step toward achieving that goal...consensus, which culminates in action.

The easiest campaigns are those within the private sector with a limited number of stakeholders. The more difficult are bureaucratic governmental campaigns with, seemingly, an unlimited number of stakeholders, but in my view, the most difficult campaigns are those when the private sector and government must work together to achieve a lengthy monumental project. The true story to be told, is a model of one of the latter when business people and government leaders achieved one of the greatest peacetime aviation accomplishments of the 20th Century. The person who broached the subject and sold the idea to his colleagues, and who has been called "The Father of the Campaign," was a young man named Bob Albin, a member of the Denver Metro Chamber of Commerce Board of Directors.

Around the world, Chambers of Commerce, City Councils and other civic groups collaborate and discuss ways to bolster long-term business growth for their city and region. The ideas are countless, and they all have the same mission in common, business growth. Most of them, it is fair to say, are short-term and tactical in nature. But once every few decades a timely, strategic idea is developed and upon implementation, dramatically and literally alters the region's social and political landscape.

The story you will read next changed the economic future of Denver and Colorado forever, and it insured the region's status as hub for air transportation for decades to come.

Without that strategic accomplishment, Denver would be far down the list of significant cities today in the United States. As you will see it is clearly a watershed achievement and is regarded as a major landmark in Colorado's historical development.

As stated earlier, the idea was proposed by a young man named Bob Albin, who was only 37 years old at the time but already a member of the Denver Metro Chamber of Commerce Board of Directors, but even only 37, he had no doubt already logged more air miles than any other person his age, and he had flown in and out of every significant airport in the world. He could cite chapter and verse the strengths and weaknesses of the world's airports, and he most certainly understood the importance of air transportation.

When Albin walked into a Board meeting during 1978, Denver's economy was mired in a recession.

Denver and the Region. In addition to being a financial center for the region, Denver's economy then and now is diverse with hundreds of small businesses and is largely based on real estate, tourism, technology, agriculture, mining and fossil fuel...energy development. In1978 when this story began, mining and fossil fuel were serious components of Denver's economy.

During the 60s and 70s Denver's economy was boom and bust too often, at times a roller coaster ride. Case in point. During that time period, Denver's energy development industry continued to grow, and by 1978 boasted of having over 1500 energy companies. But without warning, the nation's energy crisis of the late 70s, continuing through the mid-80s, sent the energy business in Denver into a severe downward spiral, and the city lost over half its energy companies seemingly overnight. A measurement...the price of a barrel of oil in the late 70s was $38. By 1986 the price of oil had dropped to $9 a barrel.

In 1978, business growth became a front burner topic around town, particularly with the Denver Metro Chamber of Commerce Board of Directors, which consisted of 35 accomplished and well-known local business people.

What to do about aging Stapleton airport, which opened for business in 1929, was a Board topic often discussed since the early 70s in Board meetings to no conclusion.

From all appearances a 1978 monthly meeting of the Denver Chamber's Board mentioned earlier didn't appear to be unusual.

But, regarding Stapleton airport, Albin, as a member of the Transportation Committee, had given the subject a great deal of thought and had reached a conclusion, and as the Board's Committee meeting began, he was prepared to make his case, and he framed his premise based on historical fact.

He began his comments reminding the group of the history of the Old World...a world that existed hundreds of years ago. He reminisced about great old cities around the world and how they developed, a subject with which every member was familiar but probably had not thought about lately, especially as Old World cities around the globe concerned Denver.

Albin told the story that members remember today, over 38 years later. He reminded the Board, "Going back literally hundreds of years, in the Old World, most of the cities that grew and enjoyed business growth had many things in common, but certainly the most important asset was having a great seaport. To have a great seaport meant infrastructure. Infrastructure meant that the great trading companies would have offices in those cities. Having a great seaport meant that businesses would flourish. Having a great seaport meant jobs and jobs fueled sustained economic prosperity back then as it does today."

He listed a number of those cities as heads nodded. He went on, "Having a great Port caused the development of roadways and highways. All roads converged at the Port. Eventually in more modern times, railroads followed. Fundamentally, you could put an equal sign between the words "Great Seaport" and "A Region of Sustained Economic Prosperity in the Old World."

"In fact," Albin, reminded the Board, "Cities in those days competed with each other just as cities have done ever since, with their port being their primary asset."

After a few brief comments around the table, Albin continued, "In today's environment, having a great seaport is still a great asset, New York Harbor and Seattle immediately come to mind along with others. And even with all the piers and docks of the New York/New Jersey Harbor...and the Hudson River, on any day of the week, ships will be lined up out into the Atlantic Ocean for miles.

But in today's world, having a great airport is just as important for the prosperity of a city and region as having a great seaport. Look at the great airports that are on the drawing board around the world," he suggested. He listed a number of them and most were outside of the United States. Were Denver to develop a world class airport, it would be an asset for developing long-term business growth for the city and the state for decades...and its value could not be overstated...just as the world class seaports fueled the economies of those Old World cities hundreds of years ago. In terms of job creation, a New Denver Airport would be a game changer," he argued.

Albin summarized, "Denver will never...until a great airport is built to replace the aging Stapleton airport, which opened in 1929 be the transportation hub of the region. Denver will never fulfill its promise and be considered a great city until it has a great airport!"

Recall in the story, Albin mentioned that cities, centuries ago, competed with one another for trade and transportation significance, using the seaport as their primary asset in the competition. In the story with the value proposition articulated, he offered the best reference possible, an add-on story that says, "This subject is about the critical importance of transportation and its impact on the economy, the business growth of a region. As a matter of fact, Denver has traveled this road before very successfully. Everyone knows the story of how, in 1870, Union Pacific had decided to route the connecting rail line to the West through Cheyenne, Wyoming, leaving Denver behind. It is a measure of our city's historical courage and initiative that caused 40 private citizens and the old Denver Board of Trade, a predecessor to the Denver Chamber, to decide to raise $300,000 in one week for a rail line spur from Cheyenne running through Denver and out into Kansas, insuring that Denver would be an important transportation hub in the region. Imagine how insignificant Denver would be today had those 40 men not taken that decisive action in 1870."

As an historical note, from the time the rail lines were connected in Utah, in only eleven months the spur from Cheyenne running through Denver was in full operation, the first train running through the city as proof.

Albin went on to explain the necessary sponsoring role the Denver Metro Chamber of Commerce Board and the Mayor and the City's government would have to play. He listed the wide number of stakeholders and important influencers among the stakeholders...land and home owners, citizens outside the City of Denver who would vote, the unions, the governor, the mayors, county commissioners, politicians, particularly those of high political office,...the press, including all forms of the media and civic groups. He spoke of all the positive support the project would enjoy. For example, the unions would be quick to support the new airport because of the jobs it would create.

Albin suggested there would be stakeholders beyond the obvious ones.

While speaking of stakeholders, Albin also acknowledged there would be organized negative opposition. He spoke of negative attack campaigns, campaigns loose with facts, which would need addressing

As he told the story he mapped a roadmap of milestones to be achieved so the Chamber could anticipate and proactively plan those events rather than being caught in a reactive mode.

Having gained the Transportation Committee's support, Albin addressed the Denver Metro Chamber of Commerce Board of Directors in the same way with the same story. Later, he would address the larger audiences representing approximately 3500 members of the Chamber, telling the same story.

Author's note: People who are familiar with the Denver International Airport campaign launching, remember that story today...decades later, because it was a true story, germane to the value proposition and creatively told.

As the weeks, months and years came and went, the story continued to develop strong legs, legs strong enough to carry a campaign for 17 years. And that, I submit, defines the type of powerful story you need when engaged in a complex Enterprise campaign, a story that can survive the long sales cycle of Enterprise campaigns.

Soon after Albin's proposal to launch a campaign for a new airport, he was asked to somehow get an accurate assessment of the future of Stapleton, its strengths and limitations.

Knowing how important legitimacy and credibility is to an assessment, Albin, empowered by the Board, enlisted fifty of the leading CEOs of Colorado asking each to serve on a Stapleton Airport Assessment Committee, which Albin would Chair, and summarize Stapleton's status as a regional airport, its expected practical life, its strengths and expansion limitations. The committee's ultimate task, Albin told the group, was to "Delve into the airport issue and reach consensus regarding the useful life of Stapleton" and, "How to reach the goal of building a New Denver Airport within a 20-year period."

Upon the completion of that survey, Albin had in hand a legitimate and credible assessment, ready for publication, a vital step in launching the campaign.

His committee's assessment of the old Stapleton Airport was echoed from welcoming supporters throughout the campaign. For example, read what Wikipedia offered …."The main reasons that justified the construction of DIA (the New Denver Airport) included the fact that gate space was severely limited at Stapleton, and the Stapleton runways were unable to deal efficiently with Denver's weather and wind patterns, causing nationwide travel disruption."

All true, but there was much more to the story.

Albin was not just proposing a solution to Stapleton's limited gates and the traffic problems caused, he was proposing a much bigger idea. His vision was one of an airport that would be the biggest and best airport in the United States, perhaps in the world, insuring Denver's position as the transportation hub of the West.

Imagine if you were a member of Denver's Chamber of Commerce that day listening to Bob Albin propose building the biggest and best airport in the United States!

Moving forward, and concluding the story of how the campaign for the New Denver Airport was born, for a period of 17 years Bob Albin chaired the New Denver Airport Committee. During the final five years he chaired the Mayor's Blue Ribbon Committee for Design of the New Denver Airport as well as participating in numerous other committees focused on economic impact and site selection studies related to the project.

As for the campaign for the New Denver Airport, eventually there would be two voting measures. Both were approved by a landside vote.

Today, spread of 53 square miles, Denver International Airport, DIA, is the biggest airport in the world, and its technical sophistication, its exterior and interior exceptionalism in design along with its practical expansion capability is literally unmatched anywhere, even among the great airports of the world.

Today, Denver International Airport, having recently celebrated its 20th year since opening in 1995, is a monumental achievement, and for 17 years, Albin was committed to its success. His management of the campaign hurdles is the closest model of perfection in Complex Enterprise Campaign Management you will encounter. The campaign was truly an artful and straight forward example of broad consensus generation, and because that is so, it is worth a summary of the framework and principles of Enterprise campaign management, and how Albin instinctively applied them to the campaign for the Denver International Airport.

1. He established a compelling, broad-based value proposition that would impact, positively, not only the Denver area but the entire state of Colorado and beyond.

2. He enlisted sponsorship for the authority to begin the search to locate the new airport from the Denver Metro Chamber of

Commerce and from the Mayor and his government at the time. He enlisted the governor for sponsorship. And from the campaign outset, Albin conducted collaborative sessions with his core of friends and likeminded colleagues, who believed the campaign would succeed. Of paramount importance, he was in constant contact with his sponsors as the campaign progressed. For example, when Federico Pena was elected mayor of Denver in 1983, Bob, already five years into the airport issue, met with him soon thereafter and brought him up to date on the campaign. Over time the two developed an enduring friendship. Keep in mind that different sponsors played different roles during the campaign and entered the stage at key phases along the way. Look at the list of governors and mayors who contributed over the lifetime of the campaign:

Governor Richard "Dick" Lamm...1975-1987

Governor Roy Romer...1987-1999

Denver Mayor William H. McNichols, Jr. ...1968-1983

Denver Mayor Federico Pena...1983-1991

Denver Mayor Wellington Webb...1991-2003

In each significant change of political leadership, it was Albin's job to bring each one up to date on the status of the campaign. Over the life of the campaign he worked at keeping all sponsors and contributors on the same page.

3. It is a fact that of all the players in the campaign, Bob Albin was the single figure who never once left the stage. The lesson… keep the campaign story consistent…stay on message, and treat each sponsor as a full partner. Keep each sponsor close by constant communications, which by definition is getting the right information to the right sponsor in the right format at the right time.

4. The assessment of Stapleton, the existing airport and its future useful life expectancy, from a purely factual perspective, represented a closed case. There would be no intelligent argument disagreeing with the assessment, and the assessment of Stapleton. Together with the promise of business growth, and the premise Denver would be the transportation hub of the Region, was a compelling value proposition and was at the forefront for the entire campaign.

5. Albin had considered the individual stakeholders and the various groups of stakeholders, and he mentally mapped a strategy for addressing each.

6. Albin was acutely aware of the resources the campaign would need for success, and those resources became available.

7. An Enterprise campaign is difficult to launch even with the full support or your colleagues, your sponsors and resources, but what makes an Enterprise launch easier and viable is having a clearly articulated roadmap of events that every constituency involved in the Enterprise can understand. Albin understood that and equally important, he knew how to articulate a logical roadmap of events. Again, every well-run Enterprise campaign embraces that component.

8. The old saying is still true, "Straight has been better than clever since the beginning of time." Straight, that is, being straight with people, straight with answers, regardless of who asks the question, straight regardless of how uncomfortable the situation might be. Albin knew that and adhered to that principle, even when he elected to meet with a group of citizens who would be forced to relocate from their existing homes to make way for the new airport. The point is: Account managers who are successful in Enterprise campaigns adhere to a basic philosophy of how they plan to confront and manage each and every event and situation

of the campaign. Without that underlying ethical discipline, the alternative is to spin facts, and, as you know, fact-spinners usually have a tough time remembering truth from fiction…and it is easy to spot.

9. Part of every successful account manager's DNA is the discipline of keeping score daily, always checking the fundamentals to know if he is winning or losing…always qualifying and anticipating hurdles. In the case of the campaign for the New Denver Airport, each event that was accomplished told Albin that the campaign was winning…one event after another.

10. As with all successful Enterprise campaign successes, Bob Albin committed the necessary time to the campaign, each and every week. Interesting note: At the time he convinced the Denver Metro Chamber of Commerce Board of Directors to move forward with the new Denver Airport, Albin and his wife, Karen, had a son, Jeff, who was in diapers. When Albin's civic volunteer work on the airport was completed, their son, Jeff, was graduating from high school. During those 17 years, every single week and almost every single day, Albin performed some task, some specific job associated with the New Denver Airport…All without pay!

Finally, since you are reading this book, the assumption is: You have an interest in what it takes to succeed in complex Enterprise sales campaigns. Clearly, the points just listed represent instruction, principles that can be learned and applied to virtually any Enterprise campaign. In addition to knowing how to manage a campaign, Albin brought to the DIA campaign, he brought personal traits to the campaign, especially two vitally important personal dimensions which every successful Enterprise campaign manager must have in spades: a) unflinching courage and b) unswerving tenacity. It takes courage and tenacity to navigate the rough waters any complex campaign encounters. The lesson here is that you will get knocked down more than once in your Enterprise campaign, probably more often than expected. When that happens, you simply have to get back up and get on with it. Again, it takes intestinal fortitude and tons of tenacity. Simple as that.

I'll repeat what I said earlier, the purpose of the Denver International Airport story is to paint a picture of the toughest Enterprise campaign possible, about which I have first-hand knowledge, and to offer a picture of perfection in Enterprise campaign management so that you will understand the simple but vitally important principles of how to conduct a winning Enterprise campaign.

Rest assured…the campaigns you will manage are those that might only last a few weeks, perhaps a few months, but by endorsing and applying the principles outlined in the story just told, you can certainly enjoy success in the arena of Enterprise campaign management.

As an aside, regardless of Bob Albin's preference to minimize his contribution and applaud others, the purpose of telling this story is to illustrate effective campaign management best practices by the initiator, the seller of the project. Those practices can be learned and applied to complex Enterprise campaigns. To the point, this story illuminates how a person (an account manager) can visualize the major phases of a campaign and how each can be implemented to drive the campaign to successful conclusion. As for Albin's preference for near anonymity, unfortunately the harsh facts indicate that it was he who hatched the idea, that he was the campaign's major private sector player who convinced influential public figures to join the campaign as sponsors, and again, Bob Albin was the single actor who never left the stage even while important players appeared and eventually withdrew. While Albin may insist that he didn't lead every charge, the fact is he was a masterful choreographer of resources, the perfect example is how he brought then President George H. W. Bush on stage in a speech the President gave in the Region, having handed the President his lines that asked for support of the New Denver Airport. And, no, Bob Albin, I'm not embellishing your role. I'm just reciting the facts!

Further Review of the New Denver Airport Campaign and Lessons Learned

As a review, exceptional account managers who win Enterprise campaigns do a number of things well starting with the ability to tell meaningful stories, factually supported, during the creation of the value proposition.

The first reason why that is important is obvious. People love stories. As you know, since the beginning of time, all the great persuasive teachers of the world told stories in order to convince. If the stories are simple but meaningful and germane to the subject, people remember them. The second reason why simple, meaningful and germane stories are important is that since they are easy to remember, the story becomes a repeatable message...passed from one campaign sponsor and on to another. The third reason storytelling is so important, since the value proposition must be broad-based, the central story has been proven to be the best vehicle to reach a wide range of constituencies, a wide range of stakeholders.

Simply put, stories are better than clinical lab work analysis and preaching.

Finally, what makes the compelling story overwhelmingly compelling occurs when an add-on story is told as proof and is a mirror image (a familiar and irrefutably factual story) in principle to the first story. Put another way, the very best reference story is an additional chapter to the story that says, "Projects like this have been done here before, and they have been done successfully right here." More proof.

This story is a vivid example of the ability to tell a great story with proof.

Exceptional account managers who win Enterprise campaigns are effective at the critical step of acquiring sponsors who have the authority to sponsor a campaign and the willingness to proclaim the project in a proactive announcement to the appropriate stakeholders.

Too, experienced account managers work hard to prepare sponsors, because sponsors do more than just introduce projects. They proactively promote and sell the project in the absence of the account manager. Also, and extremely important, they help the account manager proliferate additional sponsors who will, in turn, continue the proliferation. Each time a sponsor is added, the message, via the story, gains legs, and gaining consensus gets a bit closer.

Sponsors more often than not become strong contributors to the account manager's core Master Mind group, and they help foster additional Master Mind groups in a very complex campaign.

This story is a vivid example of the ability to identify, recruit and prepare sponsors.

Exceptional account managers who win Enterprise campaigns understand the milestone step of implementing an assessment study or survey, which upon completion totally validates the premise of the value proposition first, and second, gains and proliferates the acquisition of valuable sponsorship.

This story is a vivid example of how a thoroughly organized and managed assessment process does more than validating the value proposition. The conclusion of the assessment becomes the highly combustible force of the campaign.

The lesson of selling the assessment rather than the box, the gadget or service was introduced to me from IBM 50 years ago. At that time, IBM had introduced a magnetic tape-driven typewriter, which cost roughly 20 times more than their hot new standard typewriter, the Selectric with its exchangeable type head. How do you sell a machine so expensive at first glance? You don't. Instead, you sell an assessment of secretarial typing productivity.

In those days, when ice covered most of North America, if you asked the average office manager how many words per minute his typists could produce. Typically, the answer would be, "Most can do around 60 words per minute, the really good ones better than 90." To that answer we were taught to respond with, "What would you say if I told you your best typist can only do about 15 usable words per minute?" Eyebrows would raise.

The proof we would offer was a simple assessment, using a carbon sheet behind every sheet of typing paper for a specific period of time, which would demonstrate the mistakes made. The timely correction of those mistakes, of course, was part of the equation to determine the typist's true usable words per minute. Needless to say, the assessment process sold thousands of those machines, and launched a brand new industry, which IBM decided to call "The Word Processing Industry."

Qualifying and Resources. Major Enterprise campaigns require resources…time, staffing and funding. The assessment process is the single most important element for qualifying a project for success. To the degree that the assessment is overwhelmingly convincing, resource support becomes forthcoming, as was the case for the New Denver Airport.

Exceptional account managers know that the earlier the question of how the project in question will be funded the better. In the case of the campaign for the New Denver Airport, in the weeks that followed Albin's proposal of the New Airport idea, he led discussions about revenue bonds and how in issuing revenue bonds the users of the airport fund the construction of the airport rather than taxpayers via general obligation bonds.

Exceptional account managers who win Enterprise campaigns know it is critical to identify and address every stakeholder, be they individuals or homogeneous groups. Beyond identifying various stakeholders, in longer campaigns, key sponsors appear on the stage and after playing their part, leave the stage. During the life of an Enterprise campaign, unexpected events occur, some predictable, some not. People change jobs for any number of reasons, and if an account manager's primary sponsor retires, is transferred or lost for whatever reason, the shifting sand of sponsorship must be settled…and that is the work of the experienced account manager. Again, the Denver airport story is a vivid example of how that challenge must be managed.

Exceptional account managers who win Enterprise campaigns know how to map the logically required events ahead and the individual assignments of both the sponsor and the team conducting the campaign. Being able to articulate the event roadmap of the journey and gain confirmation from the sponsor for execution is a significant step, paving the way to an appropriate form of campaign announcement, which is a requirement for a successful launch.

I've said the campaign for the New Denver Airport is the greatest Enterprise campaign management achievement known to me. The campaign was the longest, the most complex and, clearly, a campaign with more hurdles to clear than a writer of fiction could create. For my purpose in giving you a fundamental primer on how to prepare and manage a complex Enterprise campaign, this story is exemplary because the architect who was responsible for launching the project, and who stayed with the project through implementation, either from instinct or experience, adhered to the basic fundamentals just presented of complex Enterprise campaign management.

You may be asking, "Can I do what Bob Albin apparently did in selling a very bold idea and playing a major role in the campaign?" I can't answer that question.

To help with that question, though, later in the book, I relate the profile of highly successful account managers by relating concepts which were taught in a seminar I attended by a consulting company, Development Dimensions International. The subject lists and explains the personal dimensions of the exceptionally successful account manager. As the subject applies to our intent of understanding Enterprise campaign management, it is especially appropriate to talk about the individual account manager's personal makeup, habits and gifts that ultimately render success or failure.

As an aside, as you witness the campaign for the New Denver Airport, keep in mind, you will never be required to tackle a campaign as tough as this one. You will never manage a campaign as long, as complex and as exhaustingly hurdle-laden as this one. So I encourage you to focus on the fundamentals executed in the story and mentally map those fundamentals to your own special opportunity before you.

A word of philosophical editorializing…The world is full of advisors, observers and commentators, like me, but the world has precious few "Doers" by comparison. It is the "Doers" of the world who have changed landscapes in every walk of life, and it is the "Doers" of the world who deserve our applause…day in and day out. What separates the observers from the "Doers" is the "Willingness" of the doer. The doer is simply unencumbered, unrestrained and unfettered by conventional wisdom and totally deaf to the naysayers who remain on the sidelines of life.

In the Denver story told you witnessed a quintessential doer focused on an ambitious cause, the success of which reconfigured a city and region for a much brighter future, a brighter future in fact for decades to come

As it applies to Enterprise campaign management, here is a portrait, a look at any successful "Doers" willingness.

1. The doer commits the time, whatever it takes, to eventually win a campaign.

2. During a complex and lengthy campaign, as mentioned, on the campaign stage, actors will come and go, each playing a role, some large, some small. In winning campaigns, though, one actor must never leave the stage and that is the doer, the only person, the only constant who can provide the essential thread of consistency to the campaign...from launch through implementation

3. Lengthy complex Enterprise campaigns consist of clearing hurdles, and the doer must have unshakable self-confidence, unquestionable personal integrity, dogged persistence, an appreciation for delayed gratification and a

Teflon skin. Endowed with these character traits, success is achievable. If any single trait is missing in an account manager's makeup, Enterprise campaigns can be heartbreaking and numbingly depressing.

In the world of civic project accomplishment, the New Denver Airport campaign story is a clear illustration of how the most complex and difficult of projects can be overwhelmingly successful when the private sector and the government form a cohesive partnership for the greater good of community.

Leaving the Denver story for now, here is a short story of government and business working together. Denver will always be special to my wife and me for lots of reasons. This is just one of them.

The setting…1968…Denver, Colorado, a unique city

My wife, Sue, and I had been driving two days from our home in Jefferson City, Missouri and finally on the second day had reached the city of Denver, Colorado around mid-day. We were excitedly looking forward to a few days in the Rocky Mountains, all the while, as a young couple, trying to stretch the few dollars we had.

As we approached downtown Denver, suddenly, from nowhere, we saw a police car's dreaded red lights flashing for us to pull over. Fairly certain that we weren't speeding, imagine the thoughts that raced through our heads as we pulled over and stopped, the conclusion being, "With the little money we have, there goes our vacation!"

I rolled the window down and said hello to the officer, expecting the worst. Instead, the officer smiled, looked at Sue, then back at me and began asking a few questions, like:

"You look like nice people. Where is home?" (Missouri)

"Do you come to Denver often?" (First time)

"Your first trip here! Well, welcome to Denver." (Thanks officer)

"How long are you staying?" (I guess that depends on jail time)

After the few pleasant exchanges, Sue and I got a surprise that to this day is a wonderful memory.

The officer explained why he pulled us over, "I'm a police officer, but I am working with Denver's Jaycees, and during this summer, for 12 weeks, each week, we scout the traffic coming through the city, and when we spot a young couple from out of state, who we would like to see return to our fair city, we have a special "Tourist of the Week" hosting gift we present to them. If you have a couple of days, after I explain the events involved, you will be Denver's special guests this week...all on us!

Imagine the relief Sue and I experienced! The officer then explained: "It is almost lunchtime now, so our first stop will be to a fine restaurant. It is called "The Top of the Rockies," great food, great view.

Then we will get you settled into a very nice hotel, followed by a trip out to the see the Red Rocks, then a trip to the newspaper where we will take your picture...which you will see in tomorrow's paper." The officer went on and on about the delightful things we would experience during the next two days.

For Sue and me, it was like Christmas. That first night we had a terrific dinner at Mario's downtown, a quick visit to the Brown Palace Hotel and lots of other surprises...and always hosted by very warm and welcoming young couples.

To say that Denver and Colorado will always be special to us, so many years later, is an understatement for lots of reasons, not the least of which is the delightful and completely surprising welcome from Denver's Jaycees.

Here is the question. Why would the Denver Jaycees sponsor a "Tourist of the Week" program? Answer…promote tourism? Yes, but the bigger issue is about economic growth for Denver and the region, of which tourism is just one element. Yet this story, in spite of the enjoyment of remembering it, is a story of a short-term tactical idea not a strategic program like the campaign for the new Denver Airport.

Significant Points of Review

- Sell your value proposition with creative stories.
- Gain a sponsor who has the authority to announce the your project.
- Develop a compelling assessment process that provides authenticity to the project's feasibility.
- With your sponsor's help, identify the stakeholders.
- Develop a roadmap of events to be executed with assignments to you, your team and the sponsor.

- Prepare your sponsor and mentors to sell in your absence.

- Consider your personal dimensions. Be prepared.

CHAPTER 3

WHY INVEST IN ENTERPRISE SALES CAMPAIGN MANAGEMENT?

I hope from the story told that you are encouraged, and so encouraged you will make the commitment to invest the intellectual energy to become an exceptional Enterprise sales campaign manager.

During my years as a sales manager, while focused on closing orders and making our sales targets, the much more gratifying reward was witnessing the personal development of our sales people and our sales support staff.

Virtually every time I hired someone, during the interview process, I told the candidate that employee personal development would be a mutual top priority centered around three goals:

1. Increased personal earnings year after year

2. Intellectual growth through planned growth experiences

3. Career path acceleration…promotions or career stability

When those three personal development goals are achieved, very high morale within the team is seldom an issue. Work is rewarding, and individual team members thrive on challenges. In fact, when these specific goals are consistently met, the concept psychologists describe as "self-actualization" is more likely to occur for the individual employee and for the team as well. How, according to the psychologists, can you know you are experiencing "self-actualization"? You will experience three remarkable spirit-lifting sensations:

1. You will have energy that you never knew you had

2. Time will have no meaning. You will not notice time rushing by.

3. You will feel that the experience has been awesome, and you will promise yourself to do it again and again.

So what does this have to do with becoming an expert in managing large, Enterprise sales campaigns?

When you win your first large, complex Enterprise campaign, you will experience the most self-actualization sensation imaginable as a professional. And that sensation repeats itself every time you succeed. As the old saying goes, "How sweet it is."

You can become an expert at managing large, Enterprise sales campaigns, and with your personal dimensions for growth, you certainly can become an expert in Enterprise sales, and you will enjoy the rewards of success:

1. By becoming an expert at managing Enterprise sales campaigns, your personal earnings will enjoy rapid growth.

2. In terms of personal growth, you will be able to look back on this decision to take on the challenge of becoming an expert in Enterprise sales, and you will realize that you have developed an amazing professional skill that significantly improves the trajectory of your career.

3. And finally, by being the best among the best, you will frequently have the option of accepting promotions or other leadership roles in your industry. The worst thing that can happen is that you will have gained career stabilization that

can last a lifetime. In short, you will have achieved the status as "A Pro."

Enterprise Campaign's Top 10 Essentials

From reading of the campaign for the New Denver Airport, you should by now be able to recite the 10 essentials necessary for managing a complex Enterprise campaign. But just for review…

Enterprise campaigns are expensive in terms of time and resources, as you know. There are 10 essentials that you must either have at the outset or develop relatively soon in the campaign in order to justify the time and resources you will invest in a typical Enterprise campaign. Each is vitally important as you have seen:

1. Although it may take multiple sales calls, extensive research and effective persuasion, it is virtually impossible to develop a winning Enterprise campaign without a strong, proactive Sponsor. As you have seen from the events that occurred in the Denver campaign, the sponsor, like Mayor Pena, played a key role in the campaign. So what is the difference between a mentor or a coach and a sponsor? Good

question. You see those terms tossed around in discussions about major account selling, strategic selling, etc. Simply put, you can't have too many mentors and coaches. They are stakeholders who are on your side to the seclusion of other options. They counsel you, applaud you, encourage you and sell in your absence. Sponsors do those good things, too, but sponsors differ in that they have the authority to announce the launching of an assessment, with the intent, based on the outcome of the assessment, to take ownership of a project and help facilitate the necessary actions and events that ultimately lead to implementation.

2. Good references are near the top in requirements. It is far better to introduce your references at the beginning of the campaign rather than later.

3. The more stakeholders who will be involved the broader the value proposition must be.

4. One of the most important strategic accomplishments is a clear identification of the stakeholders, and, clearly, your sponsor (the Denver Metro Chamber of Commerce Board of Directors) knows who they are. It is the sponsor's role

to introduce and help schedule meetings with those stake-holders for you.

5. The most effective proposals are based on credible professional assessment processes. Complete feasibility studies discover opportunities as well as problems. It is vital to develop a process that can withstand any test in terms of thoroughness and integrity. Tightly coupled to the assessment process is the issue of financial justification or "Where will the funding come from?"

6. As early as possible make certain that you will have all the necessary resources at your disposal. Those resources include budget, support personnel, access to facilities and access to senior management.

7. Events drive Enterprise campaigns. After reading this book, you will be familiar with 30 optional events that you can elect to be conducted, and knowing the flow of those events provides a roadmap of knowing the next stop...actually, as with any roadmap, the next several stops.

8. In multiple places in this book, the concept of how to analyze and continually qualify a campaign's progress is offered.

It is a concept that is simple but works effectively. The point is: you need a framework for qualifying and evaluating exactly where you are in your campaign at all times... one that tells you whether you are winning or losing.

9. It takes a certain level of skills and habits to successfully manage a significant Enterprise campaign. More about personal dimensions, skills and habits, later.

10. Time. The biggest investment in Enterprise campaigns is your valuable time. Only you can decide if you have the time and willingness to do the job professionally, because shortcuts won't work when managing an Enterprise campaign.

Significant Points of Review

You become a "Pro" when you understand Enterprise selling.

- Know what you need in order to succeed in Enterprise sales campaigns.

CHAPTER 4

The Personal Dimensions of Exceptional Account Managers

I mentioned earlier that you may be wondering, "Can I, with my skill set and experience, sell a bold idea to a significant organization as described in the campaign for the New Denver Airport?" I'm guessing you bought this book with the intention of doing just that.

This is an important chapter, and could have been the 1st Chapter, because it addresses the personal dimensions of exceptional account managers. My hope is that upon finishing this chapter you feel like you have been looking in the mirror.

This chapter will dwell on the specific abilities you need to develop or own as part of your DNA in order to become a superb manager of Enterprise sales campaigns.

Once those abilities and personal dimensions have been identified, I'll explain what you really need to know and be able to do in order to manage and close Enterprise deals.

Let's begin with the talent and skills you need, keeping in mind that some talents cannot be taught...they are inherited... part of your DNA, but you can definitely develop most of these critical skills.

Professional baseball scouts grade major league prospects by the number of developed tools, abilities, the player has demonstrated:

1. He can hit
2. He can hit with power
3. He can run with speed
4. He can throw with great arm strength
5. He can field his position effectively

So at the top of the heap, the best prospect is that rare guy who is considered to be a "5-Tool" prospect. Most prospects who make it to the Big Leagues don't have all 5 tools. In fact, sometimes they only have a couple of the 5.

As a hiring sales manager, I scouted sales people prospects the same way but for eleven tools...eleven personal dimensions. During the interview process, I applied the lessons I learned years earlier from a management consulting company, Development Dimensions International. The company went by the initials "DDI."

After exhausting research DDI found that the very best sales people enjoyed 10...but I added one more to make it 11... specific personal dimensions, and when a hiring organization found most of those dimensions residing in a candidate, the candidate's name moved to the hot prospect list. So in the interviewing process, I was on the lookout for the 11-tool candidate.

If it is any encouragement to you, the fact that you are reading this book suggests that you are blessed with many of these dimensions:

1. High level of integrity...Honest to a fault
2. Smarter than average...Demonstrated
3. Demonstrated initiative. Has a mind of his own
4. Sound business judgement...Loaded with common sense
5. Proven sales track record and employment stability

6. Persuasive…Ability to articulate issues persuasively

7. Personal Impact…Exudes a certain level of charisma

8. Industry knowledge of the applicable industry

9. Strong Interpersonal skills…easily likable

10. Persistent…Demonstrated ability to bounce back

11. Strong organizational skills

So there you have it. You don't need to possess all 11 dimensions to become a highly successful Enterprise sales campaign manager, but the more the better.

As a quick study, you would be right if you said, "What is new about this list of personal dimensions? Don't these dimensions apply to any sales job?"

The answer is yes. They do, but in terms of "Must Haves," for the Enterprise game, the dial gets turned up a bit…quite a bit. And that becomes abundantly clear when you have a full understanding of what the job of Enterprise campaign management is all about.

For example, personal integrity…simple honesty…is a required personal dimension for success in an Enterprise campaign.

"Why?" you might ask is it more important in an Enterprise campaign versus a simple, single buyer environment.

Answer...When a single buyer has decided that an account manager's value proposition is compelling and involves no one else except himself, his risk is limited; however, a sponsor's role requires opening his organization to an account manager, and as a consequence, his risk is far greater.

Perhaps the reason personal integrity is so vitally important is because, of all the desired personal dimensions, it is the one that is the most transparent. Totally honest people more often than not come across as honest people. On the other hand, dishonest people have a difficult time concealing the fact.

In high stakes Enterprise sales campaigns, personal integrity and credibility in dealing with your prospect is the number one impression and reputation you need to earn. The winner's credibility grade card will always register an A+ in the minds of the decision makers, so you need to guard your credibility and the credibility of every member of your team as you manage your campaign. The best counsel any account manager can ever receive is this: Straight has been better than clever since man walked upright on the planet. Being straight is transparent. So is the attempt to be clever.

If you are a straight-shooter, you should feel encouraged, because, if you are, you have a decided advantage against less than professional competition.

Significant Points of Review

- Review your personal dimensions, your set of personal tools. Leverage the ones you have, and replace the ones that are missing. Make the most of those you inherited.
- Never underestimate the value of credibility.

CHAPTER 5

ESSENCE OF ENTERPRISE SALES CAMPAIGN MANAGEMENT

To reinforce what has been said thus far... After you have convinced someone at some high level of management in your targeted prospect that your value proposition is compelling, and after that manager has agreed to become your sponsor and partner in bringing the rest of the organization on board, the campaign is underway. A couple of important first steps...

As emphasized earlier it is vitally important for your sponsor to know and list every department and the specific stakeholders, the people who will be involved in one way or another in the decision and implementation process. It is important that no voter, no party be excluded. The list might include other managers, influential users, technical evaluators, contracts, procurement, senior executives, etc. The lists can go on. The first campaign step the sponsor usually takes is announcing the assessment by either having a staff meeting or sending an email explaining in short form your value proposition and your involvement. The email asks each stakeholder to support the assessment and feasibility study in a proactive way and to communicate openly with you, the sponsoring conductor of the assessment. Here is the key point: If the sponsor is unwilling to make the announcement, taking the bold step, that person doesn't meet the criteria of "Sponsor." Here is an example of an effective announcement letter to staff.

Memo to: List

From: Jack Jones, Vice President of Engineering

The purpose of this memo is to introduce you to Tom Jackson, our account manager, who represents Advanced Information Systems, Inc.

Tom and I have met a number of times in the past few weeks. The subject of those sessions has been about AIS's system of managing information that supports our concept of concurrent engineering.

As each of you knows, we have an urgent need to insure that each of you, in the development of our next generation product, to be announced next year, receive all current data at the right time, in the right place and in the right format if we are to succeed in designing and building our new product concurrently as a team.

Having reviewed the system, its applications and utilities, I'm convinced that Advanced Information Systems offers expanded capabilities in this area and merits a closer look by you and me.

To that end, Tom Jackson will need to meet with you, individually, to gather application information, review existing programs and discuss any concerns you might have. Tom will be assisted by Bill Jacobs, who is an applications engineer for AIS. So please make it a priority to meet with the team from AIS at your earliest opportunity so that we can summarize and analyze our requirements for the coming year. Tom anticipates that your first involvement should take no more than a couple of hours, and as indicated, the sooner we complete this initial phase the better.

For those on your team who are considered technical leaders, I encourage a field trip to AIS's office for full technical demonstrations.

Tom and I are planning a trip to AIS's corporate office to meet their senior management and to get a full confidential review of their product development roadmap. Under non-disclosure for those involved, I will share that information upon my return.

Tom will be contacting you immediately, but feel free to initiate contact with him. Here is his contact information: email: tjackson85@gmail.com ...Phone: 555-221-4583

Regards,

Jack

Assuming the first couple of steps have been accomplished, the essence of Enterprise sales campaign management is all about orchestration of the resources of your organization, be it local or headquarters.

From this point forward to implementation, the name of the game, I repeat, is orchestration. In simple terms, you are the quarterback, and you are the one person who knows everybody's role in keeping the campaign moving forward.

Moving the campaign forward is all about knowing the likely events of a successful campaign and when to execute those events.

I urge you to peruse through the optional 30 events of the Enterprise Campaign Planner later in this book. In the Events Section, all the pieces will come together. Remember, if you know the next likely events in your campaign and your competitor does not, you have a distinct competitive advantage.

Finally, when you develop a campaign knowing the probable order of events that must be executed, with emphasis of key events or phases, you acquire three priceless talents:

1. You will acquire the talent of compressing a campaign, and thereby shortening the sales cycle.

2. By knowing the "Must" events to be executed, you will know early whether you are winning or losing. As you will hear me say multiple times, the Cardinal Sin

of managing Enterprise sales campaigns is coming in a close second.

3. As you become an exceptional quarterback of Enterprise campaign management, you will know how to manage a number of campaigns concurrently, and that talent, my friend, is what separates the ones who stay and prosper in business and those who move on.

Significant Points of Review

- Coach your sponsor.
- Review the chapter covering the 30 optional events so that you can create logical event roadmaps with your sponsor.

CHAPTER 6

Consensus Generation

The Denver campaign for the New Denver Airport is at its core a primer in consensus generation. Why this subject is vitally important, warranting a couple of chapters in this book, will become apparent. In the case of Denver and Colorado, the people control tax levies and increases in taxes. They vote on everything, hence, Denver and Colorado, as an environment, to get anything done requires consensus.

Where to start. If you know how an organization buys, you will know how to sell to them. Put another way, you will know how to help them buy. And that is the essence of Enterprise sales campaigns management when consensus is the core issue.

Preaching and teaching…You must understand the selling environment in which you will be competing. You must understand

and be able to recognize the difference between the old, top down (totalitarian-like) management style in companies and organizations where top down directives drive implementations, and how that style is so different from the democratic, inclusive style of management of consensus.

In the top down management environment, to succeed as an account manager, getting high in the client organizational chart has always been an imperative. It is still important, as we will have seen, but in the case of consensus generation, the mission in calling high is to gain sponsorship rather than hardline directives. Later, we will look at how to orchestrate meetings and communications with your senior management and the senior management of your potential Enterprise client.

As mentioned though, the consensus management style exists, and what is vitally important to the salesperson is to know the difference. To be clear: When you decide to pursue an Enterprise deal, know the animal and its habits in terms of style.

Let's go to Japan

When Bob Albin was asked by the Board of the Denver Metro Chamber of Commerce to look into Stapleton's status, Albin, as you will recall, formed a committee consisting of 50 leading CEO's of Colorado and postured a value proposition in the form of examining Stapleton's practical, useful life expectancy. Clearly, the objective of the process in acquiring the opinions of those CEO's, represented concurrence...confirmation of the value proposition of the New Airport. By gaining confirmation the campaign cleared a significant hurdle and is a picture perfect example of a process I'll explain in the nest few paragraphs.

Think Japan. A question...What do Mitsubishi, Hitachi, Sony, Toyota, Honda and all the other large Enterprises in Japan have in common? The answer is lots of things, but as it pertains to understanding how to sell into an Enterprise environment, all these large companies share the same decision-making process. It is called "The Ringi" process.

In short, it is how they decide things. The idea of making a serious commitment and foregoing the Ringi process is simply unthinkable to Japanese managers. In a few minutes I'll show you why you should familiarize yourself thoroughly with the Ringi process, because if you do understand it, and your competitor does not, you go to the front of the pack.

When I was in sales management, for over a decade I made frequent trips to Japan to train and develop our sales teams who were pursuing Enterprise deals. I became very familiar with the Ringi process and why understanding its behavioral rules and customs is vital to becoming successful in that environment.

So having said that, please read the following thoughts from parts of White Papers, I've assembled that clearly discuss the nuances of Japan's Ringi process.

The Ringi Process: A Decision Making Technique

The traditional decision-making process in Japanese firms is referred to as the "Ringi" system. The word Ringi in reality consists of two parts, the first being of "Rin" stands for submitting a proposal to one's supervisor and receiving their approval, the second "Gi" meaning deliberations and decisions.

The Ringi system is a traditional way of managerial decision-making in Japan. The system involves circulating proposals to all managers in the firm who are affected by an impending decision. The Ringi system goes through four stages: a. Proposal, b. Circulation, c. Approval, d. Record. Proposals are generally initiated by middle managers, though sometimes they may also come from top executives. In a "Ringi" system the ideas and plans are discussed, developed, and refined in the informal meetings among the employees. This activity of informal discussions is a kind of pre-meeting stage which is called as "Nemawashi". The key point of "Nemawashi" activity is to explain the details of an idea that is being proposed to promote for a decision to be made. This "Nemawashi" activity of "Ringi" system acts as an essential means of knitting together as many people as possible into the vital function of the decision making process.

The procedure of "Ringi" can be described in the following way: it usually starts at the lower level of management, even if the initiator is a higher-level manager, however, in almost every case he or she will give the idea to his or her subordinate(s) and let him (them) propose it. There are at least three good reasons for that. First, the first-line managers, as it is believed, are closer to the problem, and because of that, they have more information about it. Second, it has to start at the managerial level because decision-making is a typical managerial activity. Third, this is how the lower level managers can demonstrate their managerial skills to their superiors.

Formal Circulation Of A Proposal / Document – Ringi – Sho…

The lower managers are advised to refer a few routine decisions to top management through a certain procedure. He or she must draft a formal document that is known as a ringi-sho, which is usually a printed form in which managers fill in their ideas and circulated among executives for their formal approval. The "Ringi-Sho" is presented in such a way as to seek top management's approval on a specific recommendation of a subordinate. When the formal "Ringi-Sho" is ready, it must be circulated among various sections and departments that will be affected by the decision. Once created, the "Ringi-Sho" is submitted for signatures through top section heads or individuals on which all the members of the group can affix their seal - indicating in the manner of its affixing, whether they are for or against or undecided. At any stage in this process, it may be necessary for the originator of the "Ringi-Sho" to modify and resubmit the document. The indication of the approval is done by a manager's personal seal - known as the procedure of "management by stamps". When the president approves the "Ringi-Sho" by affixing his or her seal, the decision declares to be final. The role of the president in the decision-making procedure is also interesting. His or her approval is, of course, necessary but the president's decision is usually based on the approval of the rest of the executives. Final implementation will be quick because prior agreement has already been accomplished.

Formal Circulation of a Proposal for Approval

CONCLUSION... The "Ringi" decision making process is democratic in nature, with greater participation of people, and easy for implementation as formal approval is made with a great involvement of employees at all levels. For the "Ringi" system to operate effectively, certain conditions must prevail. It calls for a good organizational culture with harmony among the employees and seeks for a well-organized communication pattern at the work place. Much of the discussion, negotiation, bargaining, and persuasion are performed through mobilization of personal networks. To make this possible, organizational and physical setting must be such as to encourage regular and frequent face-to-face interaction. Another basic condition to make the "Ringi" system effective is a strong sense of shared understanding and values among participants. The "Ringi" system receives criticism for its long process for consensus, and is perceived as a problematic, one in a cross cultural context as decision making procedures vary from culture to culture in the international business. Even though the "Ringi" process is viewed as time consuming, it still ranks high in appreciation for its nature of participatory management with collective decision making procedure in an organization.

The Consensus Decision-Making Management Style

The question on your mind might be: "Why did I have to wade through the Ringi process description, and what does the Ringi process have to do with Enterprise campaign management in my neck of the woods?"

Of course, you know why. The Ringi management style, or serious shades of it, is the style of management you will find in your patch more and more often these days.

The Ringi process, in short, is the ultimate consensus management style that so many companies around the world practice when making significant decisions, so, clearly, it is vitally important to understand the general process.

Here is why knowing how it works is important: Knowing how a "Consensus" decision-making system works will transform an account manager's mental approach from tactical to strategic. Knowing the system enables an account manager to focus on the management of the events of the campaign. Knowing the system almost automatically eliminates "pressure to buy" and silly sales gimmicks...and in its place infuses a strong differentiating level of professionalism.

As mentioned a number of times, a campaign goes nowhere without a sponsor. From your knowledge of how the Ringi process works, you know that your suspect sponsor needs to inform and probably convince his manager first before proceeding. And your sponsor's manager may have to take the issue up with his manager. Imagine the damage an account manager does to the relationship if he applies any kind of pressure prematurely on the sponsor!

If you know that a potential client's decision making style is fundamentally a mirror image of the Ringi process and your competitor does not, you are far better equipped to mount an effective Enterprise sales campaign. On the other hand, if you don't recognize one when you see one, your chances of success are slim and none.

The Ringi process has been reviewed, because, in principle, it is the fundamental process Albin implemented in the New Denver Airport campaign. Let's look...

First, he generated an idea and sold the idea at a lower level.

Second, he sold the idea up another level to the full Board of Directors.

Third, with the support of the Board, he met with then Mayor McNickles and gained his support.

So far, the first three steps listed represent the initiation of an idea within the Ringi process.

Fourth, the formation of the committee, consisting of 50 leading Colorado CEO's and gaining their agreement about the premise of the value proposition, qualifies as validation of the idea. That is exactly what occurs in the Ringi process. In Japan, no responsible manager would go out to his associates and colleagues at the initiation of the Ringi process without verifying proof or a benchmark.

With all hurdles cleared, in the Ringi process voting begins... thumbs up or thumbs down.

While it took years to get there, from the original story told to the two formal votes taken, the process for winning the campaign for the New Denver Airport was the fundamental Ringi Process.

Here is another example.

In my book, Closing The Whales, I chronicle a very large Enterprise deal that we won. In that contest, we had approximately a dozen competitors. Some were very large companies with solid track records.

After we won the decision, our sponsor told us how our competition approached the sales process. He said that, one by one, each came into the Board Room and gave their corporate overview, their story detailing their capabilities as those capabilities applied to the RFP. In short they presented their proposal and left and never came back.

Our sponsor told us that not one competitor returned after giving the corporate overview for follow up meetings, and not one competitor engaged the operations people. From our competitors' actions...or lack of actions, they had called high, very high. Their written response to the RFP was complete, and, as far as they were concerned, they had done their best. "May the best proposal win."

Object lesson: Every competitor in that deal failed to recognize they were smack dab in the middle of a Ringi Enterprise decision making environment...and that made all the difference in the world. So the lesson: Learn which decision style dominates the buying environment you are in.

Significant Points of Review

- Determine the decision making management style of your potential client...Top down or consensus generation.

- Avoid pressure tactics, especially when your sponsor is gaining concurrence with his immediate manager.

- A repeat...The assessment process is a must

CHAPTER 7

THREE KEY SALES EVENTS

B efore we move on to the chapter of 30 optional events, there are three events or phases that need bringing forward, because these the phases or events get so much attention and interest in campaigns and sales team meetings:

a) The high-level call

b) Competition

c) Closing or proposal delivery

The High-Level Call….from the 30 events

I won't pretend that this event doesn't make less experienced salespeople nervous. It has been the bugaboo of selling for salespeople ever since Tom Watson Sr. hung up his spikes, but the event gets selected frequently and run with a wide range of effectiveness. It is an important event. Sometimes it influences the opportunity at hand, and sometimes it doesn't. Quite often it is more ceremony and courtesy than substance. Generally, though, if the team, which should include the sponsor, thinks the high-level call is a good event to be conducted, then every effort should be made to run it effectively.

There are whole training courses devoted to this single subject, so I'll limit my comments to a few basic thoughts. Understanding what you want to accomplish when you make the big call is the first burning question you should answer before making the high-level call. If you really get that one nailed down, you are half way home in terms of having a good call. The second general truth is to know well on whom you are calling. Senior Vice Presidents, CEO's and board members, most often, are high-achiever type people. They take the performance of the groups for which they are responsible very personally. They can tell you exactly how performance has been for the past several quarters, even years, and they can tell you what the immediate future looks like. You can bet group performance is a personal issue with them. They get up with it in the morning, and they go to bed with it every night.

The best preparation is to know the trip your high-level person has traveled, inside and out. If you know how he views his company's differentiation strategy versus his nearest two competitors, you are ahead of most, and watch out! He may try to hire you! If you know where he is headed and how your solution can hasten his journey, your chances of making a great call and winning his support for your campaign is really excellent. If you take a senior manager from your company, make sure he or she is equally well versed on the subject.

In today's world, thanks to the internet, it is easy to track most high-level executives' background, resume and aspirations. Too, assuming you know the person's title, it is easy to search the web for that title's typical "job performance and evaluation" plan. Knowing the key elements of a given person's performance plan enables you to make a more intelligent and informed high-level call.

For example, looking at a typical CFO's performance plan recently, I saw four specific requirements in the plan requesting the CFO to "Review all significant contracts to insure they are favorable to our organization." What does that say to you, the account manager or salesperson? It says that a deal is not a deal until the CFO says it is a deal.

The point is this regarding high-level calls...Do your homework!

Competitive Analysis...from the 30 events

As you think about the individual events, a fair question is whether each is separate and distinct from the others and whether each represents a separate and distinct activity or thought process.

Competitive analysis is a good example. Shouldn't the collection of competitive data be an ongoing activity, and isn't there a natural homogenization or blend of several events being run concurrently in a well-managed campaign? I believe the answer is yes to some degree. Having said that, however, there is only so much a sales team can accomplish in an hour or two with a client. Certainly, if you have conducted an Intensive Account Planning Session, competitive analysis should be a part of that session. The point, however, is competitive analysis is a critical issue and needs addressing as soon in the campaign as possible. How do you develop a winning strategy of competing?

The first rule is to understand your competitor's strategy. Once the competitor's strategy is clearly understood, the next step is to develop a plan to defeat the competitor's strategy. The big question, of course, is, "How does one know what the competitor's strategy is all about?"

A place to start is to enter an imaginary world. Pretend to work for your competitor. Put yourself in his shoes as though you were running your campaign with his product, his company. Today's web sites abundantly articulate products, value propositions, customer references and tons of information. That knowledge, together with knowing how your competitor has competed in past campaigns, should enable you to "read" what your competitor's strategy entails.

If you know your competitor's strategy, his inside mentors, how he plans to differentiate his value proposition, you are in a position to determine whether you can defeat your competitor's strategy. Again, your inside mentors are invaluable in this analysis.

There are a couple of practices that I have developed as a habit regarding competitive discussions. First, I make it a habit not to discuss or debate a competitor's capabilities with a client or customer, and I don't hesitate to make that point to a client. Second, I don't believe disparagement of a competitor ever enhanced any company's position or ever won a contract for anyone. Further, it has been my experience that serious clients won't ask for comparisons, and they don't appreciate disparagement either.

There are numerous competitive strategies you will encounter, some of them clearly difficult. Again, the objective is not to defeat the competitor. The objective is to defeat the competitor's strategy. Let's look at the campaign for the New Denver Airport and how Bob and the Airport's proponents defeated the opposition's strategy.

In every campaign, the question of how the implementation will be paid for sooner or later is one of the burning issues. In the case of the airport campaign, from the get go, the airport would be constructed from revenue bonds,…revenue from federal ticket tax money and other user fees. In other words the airport would be paid for by the people who used it.

In the New Denver Airport campaign, there was a constituency opposing the idea, and the opposition's strategy had a glaring flaw. Its strategy was based on a bogus foundation, claiming the airport was to be constructed by general obligation bonds, which they claimed would bankrupt the city. Nothing could have been further from the truth and the opposition, of course, knew that.

When the opposition's strategy is bogus, rule number one: Roll out the most credible personalities on your side and educate, educate and educate. Beating up on the perpetrators of a negative and truthfully distorted attack is always tempting, but the far better strategy is to defeat the basis of the competitor's strategy. In Denver, once the voters clearly understood the differences between general obligation bonds and a revenue bonds, from which the airport was to be constructed, the air went out of the opposition's balloon of misinformation, its core strategy.

Proposal Delivery or Closing...from the 30 events

If you have done most things right, getting the horse into the barn is a natural process, or at least, it should be. Proposal delivery is all about getting the opportunity closed, another subject that has been given lots of ink throughout the ages, much of it good, some of it nonsense. At the risk of contributing to the latter, I'll give you my thoughts on the subject of closing.

First, I have a few problems with the word, "Close," even though it is part of the title of my earlier book. It sounds like it is something you do to someone else. The connotation the word evokes from me is that there is somehow a closer and a "closee" in the conclusion of an opportunity, an unequal relationship, a winner and a loser. I don't want to get "closed." I bet you don't either. Since the word is intended to define the culmination of a successful selling effort, however, and since it is the macho expression the world insists on using to declare apparent victory, we will use it here, distasteful though it may be to many of us.

Account managers have practiced closing techniques for decades. I am amused whenever I hear an account manager execute an alternate of choice to an eager client. For example, account manager to the client, "Which would you prefer, an immediate installation or a planned-entry approach?" Either way he has bought! The sharp angle that turns a client's question into a question is equally clever to some. It goes like this, when the client asks, "Can I get in green?" The account manager responds quickly with, "Do you want it in green?"

I won't bore you with the countless, some think clever, mentally dim, verbal tricks yesterday's account managers have committed to memory and tried on clients. While some may think they are slick, frankly, I have never seen any of those techniques work. To the contrary, the only thing I have ever noticed is the distasteful reaction from clients whose intelligence has been insulted!

Here is my view on closing a campaign in a professional way. When it comes time to wrap it up, you are always on one of two tracks. One track is all green lights and the client is in agreement with the idea, the solution and the implementation plan. You and the client get the documentation necessary into the contracts and procurement groups, with signature authorization, and bingo! It is done!

There are two tracks, however, and the second track is the one with the red lights that interrupt the smooth flow of the deal. Later in this book, we will discuss fully how to deal with campaigns that stop at a red light or get derailed. For now, here is the short version.

You will recall, earlier I said four primary elements need convergence in order to win a campaign: 1) credibility/chemistry, 2) compelling value proposition established, 3) funding and 4) timing.

The account manager who uses that philosophical framework for qualifying (and closing) can identify the underlying cause of the red light. The idea is to get an accurate read on the specific cause of the red light, be it chemistry and confidence, the question of the value proposition, the financial fit or the timing. It is altogether appropriate, after hearing about the cause of the delay, to ask the question of whether there are any other reasons for not moving forward. It is very important to get stop light issues narrowed down to the real problem. Assuming a good read, an appropriate response, which may take days or even weeks, the account manager can get the campaign back on the green light track and move forward toward a natural conclusion. I don't believe closing is any more complex than that.

When you deliver the finished proposal, you should be on the green light track, having cycled multiple rough drafts of your proposal with your client and after gaining extensive knowledge of your client's process, eliminating all potential surprises. It is a good idea to anticipate what could go wrong so that your reaction gets you closer to your client rather than removed. Logically, what could go wrong? You would not have progressed this far if the credibility, chemistry or confidence were an issue. The driving value proposition must be solid to have gotten this far. The same goes with the financial fit. That really only leaves one potential problem, and that is the issue of timing.

If there is a glaring weakness in the habits of even a mature account manager, it is when a campaign stalls upon proposal delivery, the account manager having forecasted the contract to his sales manager as a "95% current quarter contract." In all likelihood, the issue quite often is one of timing. Perhaps a senior manager, a required signature, got called away. Who knows? Occasionally the reason for delay is confidential, and the explanation for the stall is less than clear. There are countless unexpected events that create timing problems in getting campaigns closed, and quite often those problems have nothing to do with whether the opportunity is still on the green light track from the client's perspective. A Cardinal Sin committed by account managers is putting pressure on the client because the close of the quarter is drawing near.

To my knowledge, unless he is about to lose his funding, the close of the quarter is only an issue for the seller. It is seldom an issue for the buyer. Putting pressure on a client serves no one well. To the contrary, rapport that may have taken months to build, can be destroyed in ten minutes or less. Therefore, the message is simple: Deliver the finished proposal assuming you are on a green light track, and you probably are. Good sponsors, good clients, don't like to surprise their business partners like you, so expect the best. If it turns out otherwise, your sponsor, your client, may have been surprised as well, so keep your chin up and respond the way you would if the roles were reversed between you and your client. The idea is to stay alive and stay healthy with your sponsor and your client, and partner with him another day. If you handle it right, your relationship with your client will get tighter.

Significant Points of Review

- The high-level call is most effective when thorough homework has been conducted regarding the potential client.
- Understand your competitor's strategy, and determine how you can defeat his strategy.

- Wrapping things up is a natural process, assuming the previous events have been executed professionally and harmoniously. Focus on the four key elements: credibility, value proposition, funding and timing. When those four converge, the deal is done.

CHAPTER 8

30 OPTIONAL ENTERPRISE CAMPAIGN EVENTS

The events of an Enterprise sales campaign was first introduced in my short instruction book, <u>Closing the Whales</u>. In terms of basic content, along with the anecdotal stories used to reinforce the major point being presented, the value has not changed; therefore, I've included the events of a campaign here.

It is appropriate to point out that the following optional 30 events apply to sales involving a product or service, so if the campaign is a campaign to build an airport or other public project, for example, a few of the events are not applicable. Having said that, most are relevant to any serious Enterprise campaign.

It is no exaggeration that ninety percent of the account managers who make their living in lengthy sales campaigns manage those opportunities in a reactive mode at least two-thirds of the time. This concept will help you understand the sales campaign journey, how to create momentum, and you will know, intimately, the predictable stops along the way. Being able to see an entire Enterprise campaign roadmap, brightly illuminated, from start to finish, is a decisive competitive advantage over a competitor who drives his campaign as though he were in a blinding rain-storm. Being able to predict the stops is a huge part of the answer of creating campaign momentum!

The central idea is to understand how the campaign is likely to unfold, the flow of the engagement. It is about having far more events in your tactical portfolio than your opponent and knowing when to execute those events. It is about executing all the events that must be conducted, leaving nothing to chance. In the business of running Enterprise sales campaigns, it is about right tactical moves at the right time, thereby compressing the time it takes to get opportunities done. As every account manager knows, the business of staying in business is about having several campaigns moving forward concurrently, making the law of big numbers work for you.

Finally, and arguably most important, as emphasized repeatedly in this book, it is critical for you and your team to be working on only qualified opportunities, opportunities that have a good chance of happening.

As you scan through the events, you will be disappointed if you expect a new, startling revelation. For example, the idea of acquiring an inside sponsor has been around for decades, but it is seldom deployed to its full advantage. Developing differentiation is another example of an old concept that seldom gets achieved. The point is this. The value of the framework of events will help immensely in anticipating likely events and as a result, quicker preparation and more effective execution will be competitive advantages for you. This concept is like a map for the journey of the campaign for the sales team and the client. The events are like stops along the way. Keep in mind, they are all optional and not necessarily in chronological order.

EVENT NUMBER 1

FEASIBILITY AND ASSESSMENT

S tanding a bit back, in this book we have labored on the subject of conducting the assessment. Frankly, though, the value of conducting a thoroughly professional assessment at the beginning of an Enterprise campaign cannot be overstated.

To make the point further, if I were put in charge of a sales team today, a sales team with Enterprise opportunities on the horizon, one of the first things I would do: I would gather my staff and create a very thorough assessment tool, and from my view, if the extensive nature of the assessment reached the point of over-kill, that would be just fine with me.

You see, if you conduct the first event right, not an optional event, and execute fully, you will gain momentum and a significant differentiating advantage over all your opponents. Your strategy for your first meeting should be to gain confidence and the all-important credibility with the potential client, to get the chemistry stirring in a positive motion. The right way to begin is by you asking the right questions rather than you showing up with all the right answers.

Mack Hanan, a well-known sale trainer, who is credited with being the Father of Consultative Selling, wrote a book on the subject over thirty years ago, and IBM, among others, subscribed to Mack's training and applied the concept religiously.

What are the principles of consultative selling? Simple! Adequate analysis and patient examination before prescriptions get written! Think about it. If you knew you had a health problem, with no clue of the cause, how would you feel about a doctor who immediately prescribed treatment without a reasonable examination? The same lack of confidence results when account managers proclaim value propositions without examination.

Our first event should be a chapter out of Mack Hanan's book. During IBM's heyday, when IBM controlled the mainframe business, almost without exception, whenever a new opportunity developed, the branch office always suggested a feasibility study, a full exploratory survey of existing systems, customer and user objectives, problems, potential solutions, existing costs, maintenance issues, service priorities, etc. Talk about building credibility! The best first step in developing great chemistry is to first build great trust.

One of the most difficult challenges in successfully managing large, Enterprise campaigns is establishing clear, attractive differentiation. How the assessment phase is established and pursued can be the real differentiation among the competing vendors.

Do the right thing by the customer and trust and credibility will follow. So will momentum! That, by the way, is the correct order of things. As trust and credibility become established, it becomes more natural to get a clearer picture of the central qualifying issues, such as:

- The real decision-makers
- Schedule for decision and implementation
- Key criteria issues from the potential client's perspective
- Availability of funding
- Our ability to deliver a differentiating value proposition

Reality dictates that in order to engage long-term with any prospective client, the importance of sound qualifying, like conducting the assessment, cannot be overstated. Conducting the right level of assessment affords this important step.

Case Study

I worked with an outstanding account manager years ago. His name was Scott.

Our company sold software to the electric design engineering community. Before presenting solutions to any client, Scott would have more knowledge of the client's environment than anyone calling on the account. For example, if the client's potential were printed circuit board solutions, Scott would know everything about the client's parts management program. Scott would know the number of turns (repetitive efforts for electronic routing and timing closure) in getting boards finished and confirmed by the client. Scott would know their design and simulation system, and he would understand the targeted system of the board, the application of the full system, the number of layers, the size of the boards, the thermal requirements, the type of mounts

106

required, the specific past routing problems and countless other valuable pieces of information that would put him in a position of strength with his client.

Scott would get all this information simply by asking for the client's cooperation in gathering information, a feasibility study. Put yourself in his opponent's shoes. If you didn't have the same information, how would you like to compete against Scott in that scenario? Not I! And oh! Another thing. I never once saw this outstanding account manager try to outsmart a customer. Instead, he was very much into "doing the right thing by his customer! Did Scott also understand campaign momentum? You bet he did!

Another Case Study

A major consulting organization in Asia had landed a huge contract for completing the architecture and application development for a major customer. The contractor jumped on the project immediately, put a project manager on site, hired dozens of independent software companies for writing code and off they went. One of the critical requirements of the contract was that the system be developed in a specific programming language. The major contractor in this case learned quickly how little it knew about the designated language and the architectural development phase. To make a long story short, within nine months the company tried six different project managers in an effort to get the program on track.

The customer was furious with the contractor, and the contractor was bound, financially, to perform.

My company was a vendor of software development technology, based on the language of choice, and we had a consulting services team with expertise in the application development process. We were invited by the contractor to submit our license pricing for the project. Typical entry into a high-tech campaign! To make it even more typical, they asked for a corporate overview of our company and a full-scale demonstration. We knew we had a significant Enterprise deal before us if we did a few things right.

Did we have a corporate overview? Absolutely! Could we do demonstrations? You bet, with the best! Would that have been the best thing to do for the customer? Not hardly! Further, it would not have been the best thing to do for the organization I represented.

What we countered instead was to have one of our consultants join me for a period of two weeks on site to conduct a feasibility study in order to provide some useful counsel and perhaps a proposal, including software license pricing. We also said we might not participate unless we were sure our participation in the project was going to be successful

We were given the green light to move forward with the right level of access to all the information we needed to gather.

At the conclusion of the two-week period, thanks to our exceptional technical consultant and a superb inside friend, a long-time employee of the contractor, we knew far more about the project than the contractor or the customer. We knew how to get it on the right path, the scope of the architectural problem, the priorities of the project management team and a good estimate of the number of applications that could be developed within twelve months.

When we summarized our findings, we proposed that we develop the architecture with bundled software and maintenance.

In short, the prospect was on our side as was our internal sponsor. Also, after spending two great weeks with our consultant, there was no way the project manager was going to watch us walk away. We won a multi- million dollar contract to develop the architecture, which we completed in ninety days-set up by executing the diagnosis or assessment event at the right time and under the right circumstance. An account manager will make a positive impression on the client by not rushing to conclusions and solutions. Rather, by approaching the opportunity as a professional, as a consultative account manager and not looking like someone who needs to close one more deal quickly in order to make his target for the current quarter, a positive impression will be made. Don't misunderstand and think that we are going to make a career of studying and analyzing our client. We don't want to overdo the feasibility phase. On the other hand, in order to approach our customer as consultative account managers, a reasonable level of due diligence is necessary. Put another way, whoever wins this campaign will excel in the diagnostic due diligence phase, the feasibility phase, of managing the campaign. Let me ask you. Assume two account managers from competing companies have the same opportunity. They call on the same client, and one asks for the opportunity to conduct a due diligence survey or an assessment.

The other schedules a demonstration and corporate overview for the next activity, which happens quite often. Of the two, on whom would you place a serious bet? Which one has gained trust, credibility and momentum?

EVENT NUMBER 2

DIFFERENTIATING POSITIONING WITH REINFORCEMENT

The objective at the outset of the campaign is to gain credibility and unique positioning. Establishing position, how we want the client to view us from this point forward, is of paramount importance. Positioning is another word for differentiation. However, it is more than differentiation. Great unique positioning means attractive, compelling differentiation. You can't win without it.

How do you gain positioning?

Closely tied to the first event, the assessment phase, positioning and gaining differentiation, is more about teaching the potential client about the fundamental differences inherent in large, complex campaigns versus those on a minor scale and why the assessment or diagnostic phase should be much more thorough and unhurried. Once the client understands and supports the idea of serious investment into all the realities associated with complex opportunities, best positioning and best, attractive differentiation will have been established. If this vital step is shortchanged, we will probably look the same as our opponent to our client. In fact, if we are unable to establish genuine unique positioning-attractive, compelling differentiation, then our client has no reason to see us differently, and we will end up competing on price.

Another objective we must accomplish with the execution of Event Number Two is hard evidence that we can deliver on the value proposition. It has been said that once you offer your value proposition, if you don't have three clients who are willing to swear on a stack of Bibles that you are telling the truth, you are really not in business quite yet.

The good news about the objectives of Event Number Two is the issue is binary. We can either differentiate ourselves or we can't. We do either have a value proposition that we can prove or we can't. If we can in both cases, we should go forward with high expectations. On the other hand, if we can't, why spend resources on a campaign that isn't likely to go anywhere?

EVENT NUMBER 3

THE VALUE PROPOSITION

I n the sales process, value propositions range from generic, broad, general value propositions to the ones that really count: the customer- specific, campaign-driving value propositions. The objective of Event Number Three is to establish a value proposition with our client that will be strong enough to survive and drive the campaign through conclusion.

The language of business is money. True value selling equates to putting a customer-specific, legitimate dollars and cents value proposition on the table that is compelling to your client. I would hasten to add, though, it is nearly impossible to develop a legitimate value proposition without the help of the client, without the client's support and involvement. In fact, from the due diligence conducted in the first event, and, now, with our client's help in structuring the value proposition, we are being told exactly how to write the proposal.

If you are looking for truisms, here is one that is nearly Gospel: If your client doesn't help author your proposal, your odds on doing business are very slim. A compelling financial value proposition generates momentum like nothing else!

EVENT NUMBER 4

THE CAMPAIGN SETUP SCHEDULE

If we have accomplished our mission so far, whether in one meeting or more, the next event is to set up several significant events in one five-minute client conversation. This is a suggestion to a reasonable schedule of events required for any serious engagement. If we do this one right, you and your customer come out ahead. The goal is to establish a number of events with a logical schedule that your client agrees to support. Some of the key events that need calendar coordination are:

1. Corporate overview to a larger audience
2. Breadth and depth participation strategy
3. Technical presentations
4. Perhaps benchmarks
5. Reference checking and visits

6. Configuration development

7. Proposal preparation Requisition development

8. Order placement

9. Training

10. Site preparation

11. Installation

You may think this is a real stretch to suggest a calendar date for each of the events just mentioned, but that is exactly how the best professionals structure this phase, the objective being to setup the balance of the campaign under the most favorable of circumstances.

Keep in mind, only three people will ever establish the rules of engagement: Your client, your competitor or you.

You might be thinking, "Wow! What a big gamble so early in the game!" Congratulations! That was exactly my reaction the first time I was introduced to this concept many years ago. However, if we lead the conversation with our client along these lines, more likely than not, we will be viewed as confident and professional. After all, if we were about to enter an agreement to build a building for our client, this is exactly the conversation we would be having. If we were re-designing the interior of his office, this is the conversation we would be having. If we were responsible for developing and producing their annual convention, this is the conversation we would be having, so why would we not be having this conversation since we are discussing a significant situation for them as well as ourselves? We would, and it is just that simple.

We are demonstrating that we know how to do this and that we have done it before. Confidence in us should be rising. Proof builds confidence even more. Getting the references setup is a confidence builder. We, therefore, have impacted the most important element, credibility and confidence, in a number of ways. The value proposition, with proof, can only increase that confidence. The calendar of scheduled, and mutually agreed upon events, will compact the campaign, and the proposal preparation initiates the closing process. This is a key conversation, and either recruits our client to being a co-partner in our campaign or the conversation gives us direction for our next management decision.

Case Study

The company I represented provided secure, private web sites for companies who were taking advantage of the power of the web as communications and marketing vehicles and for companies that were planning e-commerce implementations.

We had been working with a company, and our technology was a good fit for their requirements. However, they were very bureaucratic in their decision-making process. We executed Event Number Four.

We had gained differentiating positioning, then presented the multi- event acquisition and implementation schedule to the internal project manager, and he, in turn, presented that same schedule, word for word, which included placing the order, to the decision-makers of the company. The project gained their blessings, and we won the opportunity.

Another Case Study

I worked with an applications engineer turned account manager named Paul, who managed an Enterprise campaign, working with a major aerospace company in Southern California about implementing a concurrent engineering environment. He conducted a masterful job of the feasibility study, and the documentation was so complete, so full of facts, that, without question, Paul and his consultant partner, Van, knew more detail of the requirements than the customer. Without spending excessive resources, they thoroughly understood every corner of their engineering environment. When the time arrived for them to present the schedule of events to the client, they had total trust and influence with the key people.

EVENT NUMBER 5

ACQUIRING A SPONSOR

I can't recall ever winning a campaign or from the sidelines watching an account manager win a campaign without the help and support from a sponsor, or in very larger opportunities, several mentors inside the client's inner circle.

I don't believe it is possible to win large, complex campaigns without mentors from the inside helping the account manager and guiding him through the organization. In fact, if you are ever in trouble in a campaign, the first rule, always, is to sit down with your sponsor or mentors and listen as hard as you possibly can. So our fifth event must focus on finding our customer sponsor, which, by the way, may not be easy.

The real definition of the word, "sponsor," is that he must be "only your sponsor" and totally on your side and want you to win to the exclusion of all other options, including internal competing options. It is easy for an account manager to find people who will hand out information, and occasionally, valuable information. Having a sponsor, though, makes all the difference in the world. What does the profile of a winning sponsor look like?

Earlier you saw the six dimension of the ideal sponsor. Since the sponsor plays such a key role, here are further thoughts about our best ally in an Enterprise campaign. In profiling a sponsor, look for someone who is inside the block of influence that exists in every organization. Look for someone who has persuasive instincts, a talent for presenting ideas. The last person you want is a person who is at odds with key people inside the client's environment, and one who would find it difficult to sell American-made cars in Detroit. The dimension of an ideal sponsor is someone who not only is inside the buying organization's block of influence, but someone who is assertive, someone who can sell on your behalf when you are not there, someone who can defend your value proposition on your behalf.

Most of us, as account managers, when an opportunity is finally closed, feel that we got it done. I'm afraid not! The selling process goes on whether we are present on the client's site or not. Most of the time, when a significant organizational acquisition occurs, lots of internal selling and debate has been waged. Finally, it helps immeasurably if the sponsor has a vested interest in the solution to be installed. Those are the sponsors and mentors you should be trying to find. The more, the better, keeping in mind that in long, complex opportunities seldom will you find one person who will know who all the key decision-makers are or one person who can tell you exactly how their acquisition process works. Now let's look at the specific areas of the campaign where the sponsor can be so helpful

To begin with, the sponsor is the person who helps develop the value proposition. It is extremely difficult to develop a true value proposition without the detail that only an insider can provide. Helping get the value proposition right is step number one for the sponsor.

Step number two, as we will see shortly, is the task of developing the organization chart, users, evaluators and decision-makers. Unless you have help from your sponsor, it will be nearly impossible to structure a solid depth and breadth strategy. In effect, your sponsor needs to counsel you regarding who makes things happen versus who watches things happen.

Third, it is a good idea to have your sponsor reconstruct a previous campaign, if possible. Getting a good grasp of who did what in that previous campaign will give you a good idea of how this campaign will be conducted from the client's perspective. It would be very valuable to know what the value proposition was, how it was presented and to which circle of people.

The sponsor is invaluable in helping drive the campaign, and he does countless chores in making things happen. Getting people to meetings, keeping an ear to the ground, watching your back and introducing you and your team to the block of influence into which you will be doing most of your selling are the realities of managing a campaign.

This is repetition, and we will come back to this concept on each event that is conducted. Your sponsor, more than anyone else, can guide you in the analysis of people chemistry, value proposition, timing and money. All are essential elements that must converge, you will recall in order to complete the closing process. Keep him focused on those four issues as a member of your team. More on this subject later!

EVENT NUMBER 6

COACHING THE SPONSOR

E vent number six is all about preparing your sponsor for the campaign ahead. Quite often a sponsor who is the right kind of sponsor, one who is totally committed to the account manager's campaign, simply doesn't know what he is supposed to be doing. Typically, in the high- tech environment, the sponsor will be a person with an engineering or technical background rather than sales and marketing. Therefore, one of the very important steps is to coach your sponsor on events that need to happen, people to meet and presentations to prepare.

In Event Number Five, we discussed how important it is that your inside sponsor be able to sell your value proposition internally. To do that effectively, you need to prepare your sponsor with the tools necessary for that mission. The world has changed dramatically in the last decade. Years ago, the alert account manager would provide his internal friend with brochures developed by marketing, accompanied occasionally by presentation "overheads." Today's alert account manager develops clear, to-the-point, videos, professional PowerPoint presentations which articulate the value proposition and proof, and send it to their sponsors to help them tell the right story, as one of the preparation steps.

Today's account manager makes certain that he and his sponsor are joined at the hip in terms of staying in touch. Yesterday's account manager would make certain that his internal friend had his business card with his phone number. Usually, yesterday, he would scribble his home phone number under his business number. Today's account manager knows the value of being connected constantly to his sponsors/mentors. Both the account manager and the sponsor will have each other's office phone, direct line, cell phone, email address and caller ID. Text messages will number in the hundreds! All PowerPoint and video presentations will be loaded in the laptop, and the projector will be in hand. The supporting AE team, the sales manager, and their phone numbers will be included in the team circle. Nothing is left to chance.

If the client calls an unexpected meeting, and the sponsor needs immediate sales or technical support, the hotline between the account team and sponsor can be a campaign lifesaver.

Case Study

I will never forget a very large, multi-million dollar deal for which we were competing, one, in fact, that we were losing. We had a young sales manager who called timeout, gathered the best and most experienced sales management in our headquarters for a meeting with the local account team, who was waging battle with a tough competitor. He was the key manager responsible for the outcome, and he thoroughly understood the value of collaborative thinking. We reviewed the campaign and account strategy, all the events that had taken place, our proposal, the client's organization and our competitor's activity as well. We determined where we were doing well and where we were doing not so well.

The key question that turned that specific meeting in the right direction, and consequently, the campaign, regarded our sponsor.

We were convinced we had a positive sponsor and a guy who really wanted us to win. We talked about him, and then somebody asked the right question, "What is our sponsor doing for us?" You could have heard a pin drop. It seems that other than being a good cheerleader, our very good sponsor wasn't very active. It was at that point that we realized we had done virtually no coaching for our sponsor. We learned he had no clue of how to manage a campaign or his role in it. We corrected that in a hurry, and our guy proved to be a quick study, helped drive the campaign in the right direction and did a number of difficult tactical moves that ultimately made us the winner of that campaign. So if you are ever in trouble in a campaign, ask yourself the question, "What is our mentor telling us and what is he doing for us? Does he know what his role is in this campaign?"

Case Study

Another success story involved one of my clients who was seriously considering a new private, secure web site deployment which my company developed and sold to companies who needed the communication power of the web as a principle marketing tool.

It was clear the Executive Vice President wanted our solution. We had conducted all the appropriate meetings, given all the right presentations to all the right groups. The VP was our inside sponsor, and we felt we were in good shape, but the campaign stretched endlessly, and obviously, it was very frustrating to us and to our client as well. My internal mentor was the IT Director, and he was very open with me in terms of educating me in how his company acquired significant solutions. What was very clear was that the CEO always put his stamp of approval on any acquisition that involved multiple departments or over $100K.

Finally, as my mentor and I were trying to unravel the delay dilemma, he confided in me that the sponsor didn't really know how to tell the story effectively, and he struggled with explaining the technology and how the deployment would actually happen. Needless to say, I awoke from my power nap and realized how numb to the problem I had been. I immediately e-mailed the VP a simple PowerPoint presentation, one that captured the essence of the story, and one that included examples and proof of the value proposition. From that point we had the order in less than a week.

EVENT NUMBER 7

Resource Assessment and Acquisition

The reason Event Number Seven is a very important event is because, first, every sales organization has more than one potential sales campaign to sponsor. Second, long, complex sales campaigns can be very resource intensive. Third, no sales organization has enough resources to address every opportunity that presents itself. Fourth, salespeople must compete either formally or informally for those limited resources. Fifth, and finally, in every sales organization there is a kingpin who decides where resources will be spent. High-producing account managers know this to be a fact, and they prepare for it, because managing this critical issue early in the campaign quite often determines the pace of the campaign as well as the events the sales team will conduct. In other words, with superstar support, calculated gambles can be taken. Without that level of support, the sales team is forced into a conservative mode of management, usually from a demonstration or custom presentation perspective.

If forced to benchmark, not having the superstars in the game is a serious disadvantage.

Case Study

If Intel is your number one target, for example, and you have high expectations of rewards from winning major contracts from one of the world's technical powerhouses, don't leave home without the "A" team. A great account manager from my company, whose name was Michael, assigned to work with Intel, always made this phase a priority and understood this concept of campaign management as well as anyone I have ever known. One of Michael's great tactics that every account manager should adopt as his own is this event, Resource Assessment and Acquisition.

As an account manager, with the assignment to penetrate Intel, Michael managed many successful campaigns, worth millions of dollars, and every time, once he determined a campaign was worth the investment, he poured enormous energy and organization into the presentation to the kingpin for acquiring the necessary resources. In every one of his presentations he would have facts, facts, and more facts to support his position. For example, the value proposition will be clear and compelling. The Intel organization would be mapped with personalities and management roles. Budgets would have been confirmed. Implementation schedules would be described. Without question he was the master when it came to marshalling the power of an organization behind him whenever he embarked on an Intel campaign.

You are no better than your resources. If you have "Hall of Fame" level applications engineers, development engineers, marketing and support teams, your odds on winning go up exponentially. Clearly, your support teams do not call the strategic and tactical plays, and a world-class support team will not make up for a missed play or a quarterback fumble, but one thing is certain. If you have done your job right, and you have assessed and acquired the right level of support for the duration of the campaign early in the campaign, you are one up on your competitor.

EVENT NUMBER 8

INTENSIVE ACCOUNT PLANNING HAS
BEEN DESCRIBED EARLIER IN THE BOOK.

EVENT NUMBER 9

THE CORPORATE OVERVIEW

L et's take a quick look back at the progress we have made with the first eight events we may have conducted, and let's assume we executed well in each event. Today, looking back, we are in a position of strength from conducting an in-depth feasibility study. From that study and from looking inwardly, we structured the positioning we need to maintain through the balance of the campaign. We identified and recruited a great inside mentor/mentors who coached us and worked with us to construct a compelling account-specific value proposition. With our mentors we now have a schedule of events to execute. Our mentor/mentors have been gently but firmly coached on roles in the coming events. We have met with our own internal Kingpin and convinced him to assign the necessary resources we will need to run a successful campaign. An "Intensive Account Planning

Session" has been conducted with our customer mentor/mentors participating, and our strategy is now in place. The setup schedule established earlier has dates and appropriate action items for team members are in place

Whew! All this and the campaign just started!

Let's examine the corporate overview, because sooner or later we know we will do one. The corporate overview is a great opportunity for enhancing our position if handled right. It is equally a great opportunity to undo a lot of good work. There are a variety of occasions that prompt a corporate overview. One such occasion occurs when a client has invited a number of vendors in to "Tell their story." Account managers occasionally use the corporate overview as an introduction vehicle. In a managed campaign, however, the corporate overview has a specific purpose, and, thus, can be extremely valuable.

Going back to what we have accomplished in the short life of the campaign, what we can safely say is that our sponsor is sold. He has bought into our story. The purpose of the corporate overview, now, is to widen the circle of support. Therefore, the structure of the corporate overview has been a work in progress beginning with the feasibility study and our differentiating positioning. It gained significant development with the value proposition our mentor helped us develop. All those events convinced our sponsor, and what he wants is for us to tell identically the same story to an expanded group. He wants help in selling everyone else. That, in a nutshell, is the most appropriate corporate overview we can present to our sponsor's circle of associates who will be participating in the campaign.

It is fine to have a minimal amount of sleep-producing organizational facts, your company structure, etc. However, the focus of this corporate overview should be directed at your client's environment, your client's problems and opportunities. It should communicate the role you and your company can play to the benefit of your client, your company-specific value proposition with hard proof, specific resources you have acquired to support your client and the schedule of events to come.

EVENT NUMBER 10

THE BENCHMARK

I f you decide the benchmark event should be conducted, it is certain you and your team will be very active. It is not certain you will be productive. Too often the benchmark event is no option, particularly, if you are late getting into the game. It has never been clear to me why any salesperson would suggest a benchmark, unless his product were something like three hundred percent better in every key respect. Even then, who, in his right mind, would invite into a campaign an expensive, time-consuming event like a benchmark? Benchmarks are very expensive!

Having a clear strategy for benchmarking requires a clear understanding of the definition of benchmarking. If you are the chosen solution subject to extensive testing, that is good benchmarking. If your client has devised a competitive benchmark and informed all parties of the application, parameters, scope, etc., that is a much different question. In fact, I would like to have a dime for every dollar spent on benchmarks that resulted in the client going into eternal "No buy mode."

The first two questions, always, are who wants the benchmark and why do they want it? Third, who is writing the benchmark, you or a competitor perhaps? Fourth, is the benchmark slanted towards a specific solution? In other words, can you win the benchmark? More than one benchmark has been designed for no one to win. Finally, the last question, what is the payoff for high performance?

Philosophically, there is one time when benchmarks should be conducted and conducted with every ounce of ability you can muster. When you have a customer who clearly wants your solution, knows your solution can withstand any competitive test, swears allegiance to you and your organization in countless ways, but needs the confirmation for internal, political reasons, by all means support your client with a benchmark! For example, in Japan, nearly every significant new opportunity gets benchmarked! Why? The "Ringi" process, signature acquisitions, won't begin without it. The signature acquisition process in Japan, in part, is a risk sharing process. It is a team endorsement of a new solution. The sponsoring manager wouldn't dream of asking members of his team to take unnecessary risks. Japan, though, is not the only ultra-conservative buyer in the world. You will be confronted with other conservative organizations in all corners of the globe.

Additionally, there are specific industries where system changes are virtually impossible without a benchmark or an extended trial. The printed-circuit-board and IC layout disciplines are perfect examples of groups who require tried, tested and proven results before acquisition occurs. Clearly, methodology changes require unquestionable confirmation!

Case Study

With benchmarks, as in war, the object is to win. In order to win, as in war, you must know who and what you must defeat. Benchmarks are far more about the competing technologists conducting the benchmarks than the competitive technology, itself. This fact of cold reality hit home a few years back when my team was engaged in a serious printed-circuit-board layout solution. The contract was worth millions!

Let me set the stage. Our client was a large, potential customer who required us to benchmark against two other competitors. We had no choice in the issue. Our product was less mature than our competitor's products. Our benchmark team was new to our organization and to our product.

Our benchmark results were embarrassing. We lost that benchmark by such a lopsided score! It was more than embarrassing!

Oddly enough, a wild coincidence occurred half way around the world in Europe. Virtually the same benchmark was being conducted with my organization pitted against the very same two competitors. It was an amazing coincidence. What astounded me was we won over there by a similar, lopsided score. In other words, the entire game was reversed. The only consistencies were the products, the competitors and the similarity of the clients.

Needless to say, I involved myself in a thorough debriefing of both cases. In turned out that our key guy driving the benchmark in Europe was, first, an extremely capable layout technologist who had more than five years of board layout experience. Second, he was thoroughly familiar with our layout solution and the competitor's solution as well. He knew what our product could do inside and out. He knew what it could not do. He knew which code was solid and which code was soft. In that case, who won the benchmark? Our technologist won the benchmark! I believe this case is a perfect example of what happens when most benchmarks occur. By the way, as a result of this "Chipped in Stone" lesson, we promoted the technologist from Europe to our headquarters where we established a central benchmark team, headed by him. With him in control, we won the next twenty-two benchmarks in a row!

The lesson for the benchmark event is acid clear to me. If you have the technologists who can out-perform those from your competitor and if you are sure that winning means winning the business, then go for it!

EVENT NUMBER 11

BREADTH AND DEPTH STRATEGY

D uring the feasibility phase and with the help of inside mentors, you should have a clear idea of the client's organizational chart and the acquisition roles of each person. For example, user requirements may differ from managers, and they may not. Very senior managers may be part of the decision tree, and they may not. Direct reports to the key decision-maker may be part of the "Block of Influence," and they may not. What is ultimately important is to know who they are and who they are not. Only your mentors can help you in this critical phase of campaign management. Performing on this event pays handsome rewards. If you have the inside intelligence so that you can selectively target your audience, and your competitor wanders the halls talking to anybody carrying a clipboard, I don't have to tell you who is winning. Not knowing and understanding the dynamics of the "Block of Influence" is operating a sales campaign without a strategy.

Understanding who is inside the block and who is outside is one part of the "Breadth and Depth" strategy. The other part of the strategy is to know what to do with that understanding. For example, when the driving value proposition is developed with our inside mentor, it is vital to know that, on an individual basis, each person inside the "block" who needs to hear both the corporate value proposition as well as an individual value proposition. Let's look at some specific examples.

Nightmares and Enterprise Dynamics

I once asked an experienced PCB layout manager what his "Nightmare" worry was, and he told me. "Very simply," he said, "what wakes me up in the middle of the night is this. I ask myself the question of whether we put any stupid information into the system today that will cause one more timely, expensive and unnecessary iteration." His world revolved around schedule, and therefore, our value proposition, at the very least, needed to help him in maintaining schedule.

WINNING COMPLEX ENTERPRISE SALES

The CFO typically is a significant part of the buying circle. What wakes him in the middle of the night? Does he have a nightmare worry? Ask any CFO and he will tell you that predictability means credibility in the financial community, and he delights in announcing over-achievement and detests explaining shortfalls. His landscape is filled with financial modeling, numerical simulation. His nightmare is the company's failure to live up to the expectations set for the financial community, his CEO and his Board, and our value proposition had better, at the very least, help him "meet analysts' expectations."

The Vice President of Engineering has multiple business issues, some more pressing than others. New product development, new releases, personnel retention and budget management may head the list. Perhaps morale within the engineering team is his "Nightmare" business issue. Your inside sponsor can provide clues, assuming you have the right sponsor. The point is our value proposition had better positively influence his world.

The Vice President of Information Systems lives in another environment. Systems that crash or go down are common nightmares. Seamless system conversions make him happy. He manages the operating data systems of the organization, speaks an entirely different professional language and chooses new solutions with great care.

In my view, conducting this event is fundamental and not an option. Again, it consists of two parts, knowing who is inside the block of influence and knowing what each person's world is on an individual basis.

EVENT NUMBER 12

COMPETITIVE ANALYSIS HAS BEEN
DESCRIBED EARLIER IN THE BOOK.

EVENT NUMBER 13

THE HIGH LEVEL CALL, HAS BEEN
DESCRIBED EARLIER IN THE BOOK.

EVENT NUMBER 14

THE DEMONSTRATION

Do we really need to talk about demonstrations? I'm afraid so, and the reason is that demonstrations nearly always happen in a sales campaign, and far too often they are taken for granted, sloppily rendered and impersonally conducted. People who conduct demonstrations need to be trained on how to give effective demonstrations.

Topping the list is the need to summarize at the beginning of the session what will be demonstrated. They need to ask the very important question of whether there are other capabilities that need to be seen.

Second, demonstrations are far more effective if they are customized, time permitting.

Finally, the entire presentation should be about what the client or customer can do with the solution rather than a monologue of what the application engineer can do with the technology being demonstrated. For example, too many times in a demonstration, you will hear the applications engineer say words like, "Now I'm going to show how I can do this function rather than how YOU can do a particular function.

EVENT NUMBER 15

THE BIG TECHNICAL SHOW

Wasn't the demonstration the technical show? No, the technical show is the much bigger show of your company from a technical presence perspective. During most campaigns, aside from the demonstrations that are intended to prove the integrity of the technical solution, if the client is serious, a major event will occur that can best be described as "The Big Technical Show." What usually triggers this event is good performance on most of the previous events, although there are occasions when this major event will occur rather early in the campaign. If it does happen early in the campaign, more than likely your client has been talking to acquaintances within the industry and has been encouraged to check out your company and your solution. A good sign! Whom does your client usually send to one of the events you will be hosting? Typically, they send people in the user community who are qualified to look at solutions, those who know the other available commercial options and those who are experts with their existing environment and its strengths and weaknesses. Engineering management is often represented as well.

The people who represent the client are people selected who are best qualified to review the subject, simple as that. After the "Big Technical Show" they will return to their offices and give a report to senior management. The report invariably will answer the question senior management will ask, "Can these folks (you and your company) help us or do we need to keep looking?" That is the central issue of the purpose of the show and the campaign gains serious momentum at this point or it dies. I'm not making this up!

Here is the key point. If they come with their very best, you have to come with your very best. Typically, these folks, your very best people, don't do demonstrations or sales calls. If you have your very best with you on the big show day, the chances are your client will report back with, "Yes, we think they can help us." But if their people know more about the subject than your people, it will be a reflection on your entire company and offering, and their report will probably be, "We don't believe these folks can help us. We need to keep looking."

Every technical company that hopes to succeed has a number of technical giants who can discuss issues with the very best technical minds, and they love to do it, night or day, rain or shine, anytime and anywhere. They are the ones you want in the room when the "Big Technical Show" takes place. The problem is that the technical giants in your company are in high demand, and they are often committed to critical company missions. That is why it is so important to timely conduct the right kind of resource assessment and acquisition session with whoever your resource Kingpin happens to be.

Case Study

This is more a case in point rather than a case study. Working for a young startup company, one year we closed twenty-eight very large opportunities, each representing seven-figure plus revenue. During that run, we had one guy who was involved in the "Big Technical Show" in twenty-two of those opportunities. It got to the point that we scheduled these events around his availability just to make sure their best didn't overpower our best. We learned that the smart thing to do was get on his calendar and give him the major league prep at the right time. He appreciated it a great deal, and it enhanced his performance as well. Plus, to the client, we looked like a prepared team.

EVENT NUMBER 16

THE HEADQUARTERS VISIT

C learly a demonstration or a major technical show can be conducted in the headquarters office. The headquarters visit can consist of the two previous events and often does. Sometimes those events take place away from the headquarters. Making a concerted effort to get your client to your headquarters, hosted by you, is a superb plan. More good things happen in the extended time with your client in a relaxed environment than you might imagine. Rapport will get better as a rule. It is hard not to develop a better relationship with someone after you have shared a number of meals, perhaps a plane ride and a glass of wine or two. With good preparation, with the right people on hand to help conduct the headquarters visit, this event can be one of the turning points in a campaign. It further qualifies your client in a positive way. Assuming you are hosting a qualified client, what client would take time out of a busy schedule and make the trip to your headquarters with you unless he were very serious about doing business with you? The agenda, aside from product shows, should include a mutual exchange of information about companies, products and directions. It is great when your client will discuss his applications and how your proposed solution fit into his plans. Boldly suggesting that is not out of the question.

The Headquarters visit is an important event from your client's perspective, because, sooner or later, if the product acquisition is substantial, his boss will ask him how much he knows about the supplier. It is especially positive to have your most senior management team participate in the visit, particularly, if your company is a startup or relatively unknown. Your best salesperson can be a talented, dynamic, visionary, which is quite often the case in the management of startup organizations.

Case Study

Mentor Graphics, one of three companies regarded as launching the Design Automation Industry, was fortunate to have as one of its co-founders, Gerry Langeler. Langeler was the extremely talented, dynamic visionary personified. Though not originally of a technical background, rather that of marketing, he was without question one of the best, if not the best read personalities of the infant Design Automation Industry. Consequently, he could go toe to toe with the industry's best technical folks. Further, though never having been in sales, per se, Gerry was a gifted presenter of concepts and ideas. The point is that the home office visits, with Gerry Langeler an active participant, were virtually always central to the sales campaign strategies during Mentor Graphics' early years.

Case Study

Cadence Design Systems, in its early days, had a dynamic, young, CEO whose name was Joe Costello. Joe was a superb speaker, an experienced technologist and could dance with the best. High on the list of strategic affairs for every Cadence sales team, at that time, was to get the client to their San Jose headquarters and get Joe in front of them. It worked.

Case Study

One of the very successful companies in the 70s and 80s was Intergraph, located in Huntsville, Alabama. The key strategy for Intergraph was to get the customer to headquarters and get its founder, Jim Meadlock, in front of the client. Intergraph used the headquarters visit as a fundamental selling strategy and designed into its headquarters multiple facilities for hosting clients that was extremely impressive to any visitor. According to legend, Meadlock was a true visionary in his own right, and he developed great client rapport with his disarming but debating approach to selling his company.

Case Study

IBM built a facility called the Homestead in Endicott, New York, not far from Armonk, IBM's headquarters. The facility, among other things, had a key purpose, and that was to hold seminars on data management concepts for clients and clients' executive management. The program was billed as an educational retreat, with the participants mixing academically and socially with other senior executives, but in reality, it was a superb platform for the

Advanced Headquarter Visits, 301, a graduate class on the subject, indeed! It was very convenient for IBM's senior management to show up for social periods, lunch and dinner events. Having attended events at the Homestead, myself, I can vouch for the immensely positive impression that program makes on a visitor. They even have a nine-hole executive golf course for after-hours stress relief from the pressure of being IBM's guest

Seriously, consider the headquarters visit as a key event, especially, if your company has any capacity to make a unique impression on your client, and that doesn't necessarily have anything to do with fine buildings and putting on the dog. Now that the dog has been brought up, how would you like to have been on the competing end with your client just returning from a week at IBM's Homestead, having lunched and golfed with Mr. Watson and his staff? What fun!

EVENT NUMBER 17

CUSTOM CONSULTING

From a number of selling experiences, it seems in the technology business the idea of a vanilla, one-size-fits-all solution is quite often not the case. Probably true in countless industries. This is one of the most effective events to be conducted, particularly if your client will compensate your company for the custom work involved. If the custom modification is anything substantial, requiring significant dollars in compensation to your company, and if your client is willing to make that commitment, it is a foregone conclusion that he probably has bought your solution. Worst case, he is in the upper strata in terms of being qualified.

Custom work and services range from developing simple to complex interfaces, from added functionality to platform support to who knows what else that is unique to the potential buyer.

There are countless opportunities for custom engagements, and quite often the client will request it, making it a condition for acquisition. Equally often, approaching the customer from a Consulting Services approach is a decided competitive advantage for you. Generally speaking, custom work is a superb event when the assignment is very clear-cut, obviously doable from your organization's perspective, badly needed from your client's perspective and doable by your support team but not doable by your client. That is a mouthful, but when that situation presents itself, custom consulting is a superb event to execute. It is an opportunity to shine. It is also an opportunity to fumble. What is extremely important is to make no commitment until the right consulting person has thoroughly reviewed the consulting task, and the right level of management has blessed the project. A job well done can easily seal an opportunity, barring all competitors. A botched job can undo months of credibility building.

Perhaps a more convincing argument for this event would be from the perspective of suddenly becoming aware of your nearest competitor entrenched with your client, performing a custom consulting services assignment! Ouch!

Case Study

One company selling Printed Circuit Board layout software developed a unique approach by approaching clients through the backdoor with a consulting opportunity. Their approach was about electronic parts management to the client.

They started the conversation by inquiring about the organization that maintained the integrity of their parts library.

Most of the time, even with sophisticated clients, no such organization existed.

The next question was about the person who maintained the parts library and the integrity of the parts program. Most of the time, same answer!

The third question was about the number of parts in the parts library, and that number, as an answer, was usually between 10,000 and 20,000 parts.

This scenario repeated itself over and again, being very predictable. It was a rare exception to find a client whose parts library was current, considering that most of the time nobody was policing the old and new parts that made up the total library. Clients readily agreed that it was likely that ten percent of their parts were obsolete. The story to the client was that the out-of-date, old parts were the culprit in causing needless "turns" or layout iterations, a very time-consuming and expensive process to the clients. The client was informed that the same obsolete parts used in the design process were the same bad parts that showed up in layout, and it was the complete truth. This company guaranteed 50% reduction in layout iterations if the client allowed a custom parts management program together with installing their system. At last count, in 99% of the cases, every parts management consulting job performed resulted in the selection of their layout solution, which was a seven-figure opportunity.

EVENT NUMBER 18

CONFIGURATION DEVELOPMENT

As you might guess, a big part of driving a successful campaign is constantly assessing, qualifying and correcting. Configuration or option development is a good example. It doesn't matter whether it is a major systems change, intellectual property modification or selection of standard options, configurations that end up in the purchase order represent in-depth analysis of needs. This event is critical and good anticipation is key to execution.

This event quite often happens in a successful campaign. If you want to know whether you are winning or losing, check out the time your client is willing to spend with you on the configuration or options issue. If lots of time is being spent, you are in the game. If a great deal of time is being spent, the deal is certainly going your way.

One thing is for sure. If your campaign progresses to the point when discussing configuration or options issues should be a significant conversation, if your client shows little or no interest, your campaign is finished unless you can figure out a way of restoring life to it.

EVENT NUMBER 19

THE REFERENCE VISIT

E very industry has its own buying habits and quirks, but one thing is for certain! Impulse buying happens in lots of marketplaces, but not in the technology marketplace, as far as I know. At a very minimum, before your client issues a purchase order, he will either want to see it in action or at least talk to an existing, current user. In most seminars I have conducted, as an exercise, I always ask participants to list the events they expect to happen. This is one of those inevitable events, yet no one ever includes this event on his list. Odd, because it truly does happen every time!

Here is the problem with this event. If you don't anticipate the requirement, you will handle it on the fly. Not a smart thing to do! It is much better to anticipate, seek out your targeted reference partner and approach the issue with confidence. If you take great care in recruiting your references as partners, you might be surprised at how much support you will get. Also, even though you believe your targeted references are positive, it is not a bad idea to test the water and make sure that they will be positive references. It would not be the first time that a reference unloaded his frustration on an inquiring client.

Case Study

This lesson hit home during a very significant campaign, a large opportunity with a major defense contractor in Southern California. I happened to be the sponsoring manager of the campaign. I had been monitoring and coaching our sales team from the beginning of the campaign, which had taken approximately seven months to progress from inception to maturity. I was very confident we were set to get a positive nod. Then out of the clear, blue sky, the decision-maker said to us, "You know, this is one of the biggest government contracts in existence, and it would be a major disaster if something failed as a result of the system we are contemplating buying from you guys. Perhaps there is one small item you guys have not got right yet. We need to be certain.

Before we go ahead, I think we need to see this very same system operating in the very same environment."

Do you think I learned a hard lesson that day! The lessons you learn for keeps are those lessons learned the hard way. The story ended well because our installed reference politely told our client that, "As stewards to our stockholders, we view our newly installed system as a competitive advantage, and our shareholders wouldn't appreciate our exposing our advantage to competition." Whew! That was a close call! We got the contract, but how much better it would have been had I been a bit more alert.

EVENT NUMBER 20

CONTRACTS DEPARTMENTS EARLY

O ne of the events that will be conducted almost without exception is the contracts event; however, it never shows up on anybody's list. Perhaps it is the dread of sitting down with the client's Contracts Department, or perhaps salespeople kid themselves into believing contracts get finalized without that department's involvement. Regardless, the reluctance to get the contract issue started has caused countless millions in revenue to slip into the next quarter to the chagrin of both parties who want the contract done. There are some issues that deserve being made "Federal Cases." Sloppy contracts management is one of those issues. In addition to getting legal agreements into contracts departments too late in the quarter, too often salespeople fail to maintain control of the process. The glaring fumble too many salespeople commit is failing to address contract issues when they first come up, when those issues are often small issues. Instead they wait, perhaps hoping that the client's legal team will take the small issue off their list, or perhaps they are not aware that the deal isn't done until contracts says it is done. Not paying attention and addressing issues, though, is a major sore point to most contracts departments. Who wouldn't be offended! Too often, without paying attention to the concerns and points raised by the contracts staff, towards the end of the quarter, an eager salesperson comes sweeping into his client's contracts department and puts pressure on them to expedite the deal at hand. Relationships get started wrong and too often in a needless, adversarial posture. To compound the problem, even if the contracts department obliges on this contract, the sour taste in their mouths from the unprofessional behavior tends to linger and affects subsequent opportunities. The point is obvious. Contracts departments are not going away. Just the opposite! The message is simple. Get there early and get it done. Remember the old adage, "They can't buy from you, but they can slow you down for a long time if they have a mind to." It is like in the U.S. Army, there are things they can't force you to do, but they can make you terribly sorry you didn't. That's contracts.

EVENT NUMBER 21

PROPOSAL DRAFTING

There is a good reason why this event is called proposal drafting rather than proposal writing. This may raise a few eyebrows, but I am of the persuasion that proposals that end up as contracts are ones whereby the client contributed significantly to the authorship of the proposal. In fact, I would go even further. If a proposal has been written without draft iterations, revisions, without the client editing, I would be surprised if an opportunity is won.

The goal of successful proposal drafting is client involvement throughout the entire process so that on the day that the proposal is delivered, there are absolutely no surprises to your client. Any surprise to your client is a Cardinal Sin.

Think of all the positives whenever your client has a significant hand in the proposal development. For starters, he will be as familiar with the document as you are. Second, for certain he will be committed, and finally, if he has to defend it to senior management, he will be in a far better position to do just that.

One last point. We will talk about negotiations next, but can you think of a more natural way to approach negotiations than the process of taking a rough draft of your proposal for your client's input? I can't!

EVENT NUMBER 22

NEGOTIATING

E ven though gaining the participation of your client in the drafting of the proposal accomplishes most of the negotiation process, there are often opportunities to move a campaign along by planning a meeting with your client for the stated purpose of negotiating pricing, terms and conditions.

The immediate value to you, as an account manager, if your client agrees to a negotiating meeting, one billed as such, is that it is a terrific signal to you that you are on track to win. There are exceptions, but if your client values you and your company as potential partners, and you are convinced games are not being played, the negotiating session is truly a very positive sign.

There are lots of commercially available training courses on the subject of negotiations, and without denigrating other people's persuasions, my view on negotiating is very simple. The strength of the driving value proposition and broad knowledge of the client's situation from the assessment phase determines the position of the seller in a negotiation session. You either have a strong value proposition and in-depth knowledge or you don't. I know I am repeating myself, but when it comes time to negotiate, you are either in a position of strength or you are not.

Good negotiators have a number of dimensions in common. First, they leave their egos at the door when the session begins.

Second, they hold the relationship to be more valuable than the particular opportunity at hand, knowing that if the deal is not a good deal for both parties, it is not a good deal for either party.

Third, they are totally comfortable with the fact that straight has been better than clever in negotiations since ice covered North America, and finally,   they have a keen eye on finding common ground.

From a mechanic's perspective on negotiations, the number one rule is to have a clear objective of what you want to accomplish. Know what you want and know what your client wants. Know what you can give up and what you can't. Have a clear idea of things you can give to your client that cost you and your organization little.

In the negotiation process, though, there is a fine line between being soft-hearted and soft-headed. Treating even the small concessions carelessly is not a good idea. For a session to be healthy, both sides need to move towards the other unless either has hit his walk away point. The good news is that when two parties really want to do business together, they will find a way most of the time.

Case Study

A company I represented developed a copier device that produced outstanding hard copies of images produced from patient monitoring systems. Hospitals need this for analysis and documentation purposes.

My company offered OEM arrangements to medical systems companies for the device, who, in turn, added it to their system and marketed the system to hospitals.

The company in this case was talking with us about a very substantial order, an order worth several millions of dollars. Their contracts group clearly was not the decision-making group. The group that had made the decision was the Marketing Department of the company. The driving value proposition was the superb quality of the hard copy our device produced, which they believed would bring them market share. However, the contracts group, headed by the Director of Procurement, made it a point early in the campaign that his company expected a deep discount for the expected huge order and our willingness to cooperate would determine whether we would be the ultimate supplier. Sound familiar?

My strategy early on was to convince the Director of Procurement that our published discount schedule was final, even if the order were double the projected size of the order. In fact, without divulging customer names, I had examples of my company leaving the bargaining table for orders three times the size of the contract we were discussing, and it was the truth.

Every time he and I got bogged down in the debate over deeper discounts, I would pull out the sample copy from our device and remind him that the Marketing Department had made its decision not on price expectations but because of market share gains objectives. The driving value proposition and client knowledge is always the flag you plant when you are negotiating!

Finally, I made a concession to the Director of Procurement. I offered to take him to our headquarters (remember Event Number Sixteen) and have a heart-to-heart discussion with the Vice President of our division in the company, who, by the way, I had seen in action on the same issue with bigger numbers in the balance. I was also completely aware of what the outcome would be, and I told my client as much before we even booked the plane tickets.

The conclusion to the story is that the Director of Procurement ranted, raved and shouted obscenities towards my company. He raved against all who thought as we did. We maintained there needed to be integrity to business models, which included pricing discount schedules, otherwise, sooner or later, inequities would abound and we wouldn't be able to look any customer in the eye.

The meeting ended on a sour note, and we headed for the airport. As I let my client off at the curb, I stood and shook his hand. Then he told me, "OK, you have the contract at the prices in your schedule, but I would ask you to do me a favor, please. When we meet with my boss next week, would you mind telling him how I did everything in my power to get you guys to move our way on the pricing?" "You bet," I told him. With that he headed into the terminal. They did become a great customer and pricing never came up again.

EVENT NUMBER 23

FINAL INTERNAL REVIEW

C ommon sense would say that once you have been through the proposal drafting process and the negotiating process, you should be set to go forward. You would be all set if that were how companies actually operated. Of the companies with which I have been associated, most granted only contingent authorization for negotiating to the account managers and sales managers. In other words, they reserved the right to review commitments before putting signatures on the dotted lines. By the way, clients are no different. Usually each person representing his party in the negotiation process, even after shaking hands on the framework of the contract, leaves the table promising the other that he will "Do my absolute best to sell the framework we both designed here today to my senior management."

Sorry if that disappoints you, but that is how things actually work, with one exception. If the top responsible manager grants total negotiation authority to someone, then firm handshakes are really firm, assuming contracts are out of the way. As I said, most of the time there is an internal meeting on large opportunities for one last review.

The purpose of this event being presented is to make sure your campaign doesn't slow down needlessly. This is a meeting very much like the Resource Assessment and Acquisition event that was conducted at the outset of the campaign. It actually is a very valuable meeting to have for the sake of both parties.

It gives the selling organization an opportunity, behind closed doors, to completely think through the agreement, the framework of the contract, relative to costs and rewards. It gives the selling organization one last chance to fully review resource requirements, other priorities this contract could affect, the commitment about to be contractually made and any last-minute oversights.

The key to making this meeting a positive event is to be prepared, totally organized with all the facts at hand and easy for interpretation by those participating, eliminating a requirement for an additional meeting. The key person, besides you, is the Kingpin person who committed the resources for the campaign. If you make certain he is completely on board, knows all the details and is armed with the value of the opportunity not only for today but for the future as well, this meeting need not be a snag.

Here is the critical point that needs to be made. This event, like so many others, never makes anybody's anticipated list of events that will probably take place in a successful campaign.

Good sales campaign management is not to get surprised by any event that occurs.

Good sales campaign management is for the account manager to know six plays in advance and to plan and execute in a proactive mode versus reacting to surprises. So, don't let this event surprise you. Anticipate that it will happen, and make it a positive play.

EVENT NUMBER 24

PROPOSAL DELIVERY, HAS BEEN
DESCRIBED EARLIER IN THE BOOK.

EVENT NUMBER 25

THE LETTER OF INTENT

The Letter of Intent is a controversial event. There are account managers and sales managers who scoff at the idea of this event having any value. Perhaps they or a number of good clients have been burned. Perhaps opportunities fell flat because the event was handled poorly. There are a dozen reasons why some want nothing to do with Letters of Intent.

Having said that, there are times when the LOI is exactly the right event to conduct, particularly, if the people signing the LOI are at the right authority level, and there is a good reason to let the world know of mutual intentions. Here are a couple of examples.

After a hard-fought campaign among vendors and the client having invested heavily in time and expenses at investigating solutions, the client may want an end to vendor selling activities so that the staff can spend time and resources on the business of developing a smooth transition. From the winning vendor's perspective, a Letter of Intent, especially accompanied by a public announcement, has the effect of quieting the competitive drumbeats, and allows implementation plans, including contracts and procurement documentation, to go forward. In fact, this event does more for getting cooperation from the contracts group than any event I know. The boss has just sent a strong signal to them. There is nothing but goodness for a LOI event at the right time and under the right set of circumstances, for the right reasons.

There are regions in the world where a LOI is an expected event because of the length of the procurement process and the need of the client to have vendor commitments earlier than the delivery of purchase orders. Japan is a perfect example. A procurement document can take months to crank out of some Japanese companies. A word of caution. The right level of authority needs to be signing the LOI; otherwise, people may get into trouble.

As far as the Letter of Intent, in summary, given the right signatures, I would rather have something signed as the campaign moves along rather than to have nothing signed. Some level of signature commitment is better than no signature commitment.

It is safe to say that whenever a person of authority signs a Letter of Intent, from my experience, that person is committed. There is nothing but goodness in that.

EVENT NUMBER 26

THE SITE PREPARATION

This event is not a mundane event after the contract is done and executed between purchase order and delivery date. This event is a closing event, and should be conducted somewhat early in the campaign.

If the solution you sell takes up space or involves people's work environment, this is an excellent opportunity to get ahead of the curve. Two things occur when this event is conducted. Time is usually on your side, so performance on this task, which will definitely require good performance if your campaign closes, will be easier. Second, depending on the site preparation complexity, but the more complex the better, the degree to which your client shows interest, energy and expense in preparing the site, is a clear indicator you are on a green light track.

Case Study

Earlier I mentioned the difficult Director of Procurement who was determined to buy our copier product at deeper than published discounts. Before we ever got to the shouting match, one of the intention indicators occurred when the Marketing Department asked me to coordinate a meeting between our systems engineer and their Mechanical Design Department. The purpose of the meeting was to get physical specifications of our device so that they could design the device into their system chassis. Further, they scheduled with me follow-on sessions for actual "dry runs" of our device in their chassis. I can assure you that day is etched permanently in my memory of great days.

However, here is an equally good example of how the site preparation event is, in fact, a closing commitment event.

Case Study

One of our account managers had a campaign progressing in a state government department. The wiring for this particular system required drilling a hole through three feet of a granite wall. Drilling that hole was not a trivial task. It was more like a major engineering achievement, perhaps not in the league as building the Golden Gate Bridge, but an achievement nonetheless. The client drilled the hole long before they cut the requisition for procurement, and you can bet people heard the corks popping from our team in the next county.

EVENT NUMBER 27

THE SENIOR STAFF VISIT

Some executive-level managers are very good at making client calls. For the purpose of this exercise, let's assume your senior manager is capable of contributing to the forward motion of your sales campaign.

As with the Letter of Intent, in many cultures, it is considered good manners. It is viewed as an expression of appreciation and sincere interest in the relationship and very appropriate for the vendor's most senior executive to call on his counterpart towards the end of the sales campaign. The real question is how to turn a potentially awkward, meaningless ceremony into a relationship-building event. How do you do this?

The process starts early in the campaign. As soon as your mentor has signaled that your value proposition is real and worth the effort to drive it to fruition, make it known that your Senior

Executive is vitally interested in being a business partner with him and his company. Explain that he typically phones key people, including the mentor, to express appreciation for hospitality, keen interest, investment in the look-see, etc. In other words, set the stage for a phone call introduction for him and the people with whom you want him connected so that the diplomatic courtship begins in a professional way. Along the way, as you orchestrate your exec's involvement, perhaps he can send a note or even additional phone calls, particularly, if there are meaningful reasons.

Clients like senior management interest in their business relationships, and sooner or later, the extended relationship pays huge dividends. Certainly, when it is towards the end of the sales campaign, it is ten times more effective if the top managers know each other and have at least begun the diplomatic process of becoming good business partners.

EVENT NUMBER 28

PROCUREMENT AND ORDER

C ongratulations! By now you are entitled to feel like you have gone where no one has ever gone before! It is terrific to manage a campaign through all the events that ultimately lead to the Office of Procurement. While it would seem that the deal is completely done when it reaches the procurement office, clearly, there is still work to be done.

Without attempting a tutorial on handling purchasing agents, there are two important things to keep in mind.

First, the senior manager who made the buying decision and your sponsor, sometimes one and the same, are your strengths. Don't hesitate to use them if necessary.

Second, do everything in your power to make the purchasing agent's job easy. That means writing the quotation so clearly that nearly anyone could interpret what it says. Double and triple examine the quotation for accuracy. Don't set your company up for concessions, which result from errors in the requisition. Without implying that purchasing agents are devious, it would not be the first time that a purchasing agent issued a purchase order with a mistake, the consequences of which resulted in the order being a few thousand dollars less than the requisition. Should this happen to you, particularly, if the order is cut near the end of the quarter, you are witnessing an attempted, not-so-clever move by the purchasing agent.

Don't be surprised with his offering to correct the problem as soon as possible with regrets that the process will require several days, possibly, several weeks. You can be assured he knows your quarterly habits, and many see it as part of their job to shave bucks off of purchase orders when it can be done easily with the help of a desperate sales organization. From their view it is just good, clean fun.

The best way to manage procurement is face-to-face with expectations set from your mentor with you present, and it doesn't hurt for your sponsor to remind the purchasing agent to call him at the first sign of any problem.

Having cautioned you about the very small minority of purchasing agents who attempt unethical stunts on unsuspecting account managers, my own experience has been very positive with that profession. I believe that the vast majority of them come to their jobs with the intent to serve their companies and suppliers with competence and integrity. That is as politically correct as I can get it.

EVENT NUMBER 29

CUSTOMER TRAINING

There is an old saying that an opportunity is never quite done until the customer has paid, and the check has cleared. There is wisdom in that expression, so, that by itself would motivate any account managers to stay on top of the details like customer training on a timely basis.

Like many of the events that at first appear part of the detail of managing the acquisition process, customer training can be a resourceful approach to getting customer commitment to your solution. Just because customer training normally takes place just before installation, that doesn't mean it can't be used as a convincing vehicle. In a fierce, competitive battle, there is nothing wrong with having the user community on your side, so if you know for certain that you solution is substantially more user-friendly, then consider conducting this event during the battle rather than at the end. This event, too, if the client agrees to it, is a very positive signal that your campaign has good momentum.

EVENT NUMBER 30

DELIVERY

High-producing account managers know the importance of emphasizing delivery as a major event. How the solution gets delivered sets the tone, the atmosphere, the foundation for the relationship going forward, and how the solution gets delivered has everything to do with the follow-on business.

If the support people are on hand when delivery happens, and the solution is delivered with care, with the user community properly trained and the site properly prepared, you are off on the right foot.

Reference selling works in most businesses that I know of, and the intent with most account managers is to grow clients and territories geometrically rather than from one at a time. Right delivery habits hasten that process!

Case Study

At the beginning of the design automation industry development, we had a number of accounts that started with one workstation. We poured every ounce of effort into making that single workstation a bright example, knowing that the one would lead us to three others, and that, in fact, is what happened. Then we worked with the same fervor to insure success with those three. Those three would lead to nine or more. Four years later in many instances, our company had hundreds of stations installed, and they all started with just one.

Do a great complete job on delivery. Make the first delivery a major event in everyone's mind to the degree that you can and you will never be sorry.

Event Framework Summary

In order to be able to think six steps ahead of your competition, you must know what the next six steps of a campaign are.

As I said earlier, all the events detailed in the "Event Framework" don't happen in every campaign. Some are fundamental and in some way take place, whether prompted and managed by the salespeople or not. Others are clearly optional. The idea is to be able to see a full campaign at a glance and to be able to quickly decide what does and does not make sense at a particular time in the campaign. As important as anything, I feel, as I said at the beginning, if you have ingrained a solid concept for qualifying and closing, you will always be headed in the right direction, and right direction is ninety percent of the battle.

Depending on the situation at the moment, depending on the person, place or thing happening, the key is to be in a constant state of correction to keep the sales campaign on course, like a guided missile. The key is to understand the pattern and profile of a successful campaign, and the achievers among salespeople know that pattern, that journey, like their hometown neighborhood. They know how to think six steps ahead of their competition, because they know what the next six steps are in the process.

Significant Points of Review

- Identify those events that are germane to what your campaign involves. If you are selling a product or service, nearly all the events described are applicable. If you are promoting a project like the New Denver Airport, clearly, some are not.

- Knowing the logical sequence of events to execute is the hallmark of a proactive and effective account manager as opposed to one who is always in a reactive mode of operation.

CHAPTER 9

REVIVING STALLED CAMPAIGNS AND REGAINING MOMENTUM

N othing is more frustrating to an account manager or sales team than having a campaign stalled. Especially if the reason is not obvious!

When a campaign stalls, the sales manager starts losing patience, starts asking all sorts of questions, and guess what? The Far East doesn't have a corner on the loss of face market! Loss of face can occur in countless places! At home! At the office! At the bank! You name it!

The best cure for stalled campaigns is prevention! I wouldn't blame you if you think this is too dogmatic, but I believe, as I have said repeatedly, the best sales campaign management begins with a clear understanding of those four elements (credibility, compelling value proposition, funding and timing)

Which need to convergence to get an opportunity completed.

The secret to being a great closer is all about moving things in the right direction. It is about those four potential directions of conversations between you and your client, four potential directions events might take, four broad directions needing resolution from your client's perspective. Therefore, you must have a process that constantly gives you accurate direction, a process that works. If you ingrain this process, always being headed in the right direction, as your starting point, you will be on the right path to winning the larger opportunities.

The stalled campaign puzzles most salespeople. The quick answer to a stalled campaign is to create an event. The more important issue, however, is to be certain that the event being created is the right one, and that depends completely on your analysis of which broad condition needs to be fixed. Your qualifying process determines all of this.

The thought process we have been discussing will not only serve as a quick and conclusive qualifying process, it will anchor and keep you on track to a successful conclusion in your sales campaign, or it will hasten your exit from the campaign before you waste precious resources.

The skill of qualifying is not a graded skill as in school where students earn A's, B's or C's, etc. In the practical world of large opportunities, long sales cycle management, the skill of qualifying opportunities is binary, pass or fail. As mentioned earlier, if there is a cardinal sin committed by account managers in the long, complex campaign arena, because campaigns are so long and so expensive, it is finishing a close second.

Assessing campaigns in process and knowing how to break through a stalled campaign is an issue of understanding the difference between "Yes" and "No." Handling "Yes" is not a problem. It is the "No" part that gives us problems. We all know what "No" sounds like, but what you need most when you hear "No" is direction. It is easy to get lost in a campaign, like being lost in a wilderness with no clue of which direction to turn. What is needed most if you are in the Northern Hemisphere is a compass, because a compass will give you "True North" bearing. Having a directional process in campaign management that gives you certain "True North" bearing is a priceless skill to acquire. When you acquire this skill you no longer gamble your time or the resources of your organization.

Early in this book the major differences between very large, complex opportunities and those much smaller in scale were outlined. Understanding those differences is critical. Also in large part, the premise of this book is on two other foundations. One, the journey of any specific campaign has far more stops or events than most salespeople can predict. Two, high-producing salespeople adhere to a specific set of qualifying principles, adjusting their actions to conform in a course-correcting, cybernetic guided behavior.

Here is the fundamental truth to accurate qualifying and getting a stalled campaign back on track. Ready for dogma?

Again, there are only four directional conditions or reasons why you will ever lose an opportunity or have one stall! Only four!

On one side of the coin, any one of the four can cause blockage to successful closure. On the other side of the coin, all four elements must converge to win the opportunity.

The first reason campaigns stall or die is because of the lack of credibility and good chemistry at the right level. The right level means all levels involved with the decision. There are those who believe that credibility, by itself, is enough. Not so. Credibility is essential, but the client must feel good about you, your company and your solution up and down and across its organization. As discussed earlier, in large, complex opportunities the number of decision-makers and key influencers is a much bigger number. The credibility and chemistry issue is a tough problem, because most people won't tell you that they don't trust you, or that they don't like you. If they have had problems with your organization in the past, they may be reluctant to share that with you. People move around more often these days, moving from one opportunity to another, and they typically take their baggage with them. The problem with objection number one is that it is the silent objection all too often.

The second reason campaigns stall or die is because the value proposition being promoted by the sales team is not compelling or lacks attractive differentiation. There are a lot of value propositions that are good. Sometimes they are just not good enough. They must be compelling and different enough to justify action and the courage to act on the part of the client, who usually has to do a significant amount of internal selling before the contract is finally done. What this objection is about is whether your client believes that your solution is better than the existing condition, and if it is better, is it better than other alternatives open to the organization? At the same time, if there are internal competing elements for limited funds, your value proposition must also win over other campaigns being waged that, ordinarily, have nothing to do with your proposal. The second objection, however, is still the question of compelling and differentiating value proposition.

The third reason campaigns stall or die is because of timing. Simply put, for whatever reason, and the reasons are endless, this day, this week or this month is just not the right time. To be sure, sometimes with enough creativity and ingenuity, the selling team can take this problem off the table. The effort should certainly be made if the client is willing to cooperate. There are a couple of problems with the timing objection.

First, sometimes the client will have reasons for not telling you there are timing issues, and it may be inappropriate for you to continue down this path of convincing as though there are no problems.

The second problem with the timing issue is to quickly recognize it as such and determine whether the problem is personal or one that can be fixed with a little creativity. One thing is for certain, though, countless opportunities are lost and countless good relationships jeopardized because an amateur sales team ran into the roadblock of timing and tried to bulldoze its way through it!

The fourth and last reason campaigns stall or die is because of funding issues. In other words, the client doesn't have the money, or the price is out of line in the client's mind. Another way of putting it: your financial proposal doesn't mesh with your client's requirements.

So again there you have it! Those are the only real roadblocks you will ever have to overcome, regardless of what you are selling, simplistic though it may sound. True, they are all tough and difficult to deal with when confronted. There are two pieces of good news, though. If you know you can bring all four elements to convergence, then you have the justification to gain all the resources necessary from your company as well as those of your client in order to win the opportunity. The other piece of good news is that the sooner you conclude you can't make those four elements converge, the better off you are.

Great account managers are always, without exception, great qualifiers, as said several times in this coaching session, and if they know there is no opportunity they can win, they get out early. They are profitable to their companies. They are the favorites of the AEs and the engineers. Amateur salespeople run long campaigns. They exhaust untold resources, hang in there until the last dog is dead, and most of the time, finish a close second in the race. That might be okay if it were horse racing, and they paid the top three finishers, but it is not okay if you are running a sales campaign.

There are at least six additional reasons to ingrain the qualifying presented here.

First, using the process will help guide your decisions on the specific events of your sale campaign. You will make better decisions on which events should be conducted and in what order those events should occur. You will do a more complete job of covering the account, upper and middle management, as well as the user community, if appropriate.

Second, you will hear objections more clearly. Your listening will be focused and tuned to categorizing significant points made by your client. You will plug what your client says into the appropriate issue.

Third, because your listening will be better, you will be on the same wavelength with your client. In other words, you will be hearing what your client is feeling and thinking, not necessarily what he is actually saying. Your interpretive skills will be on the bullseye more often than not.

Fourth, with your listening and interpretive skills at higher levels, you will be able to respond to the appropriate issue instead of guessing which direction to take the conversation, and consequently, the campaign. If you guess right, you are okay. If you guess wrong, there is no guarantee you can get things back on track.

Fifth, as you move through the campaign, you will have a better feel for where your competitors are performing well or not so well. Using the compass concept as an analytical process will give you a competitive advantage.

Sixth, if your campaign gets bogged down, the process is the very best tool as a point of origin in determining where you are at the moment in the campaign. You either have a relationship problem, a value proposition issue, a timing problem or a money question that needs resolving. One of those four! If you don't believe me, try this as an exercise with your fellow account managers. Gather them into a conference room. Draw a quadrant and label each quartile (chemistry, value proposition, timing and money). Now have your fellow teammates list every objection they have encountered during the past three months as you put those objections into their appropriate quartiles. I promise you that you will only need the four quartiles to list all of their objections. Additionally, you will be able to categorize every lost campaign using the same process.

How do you get a stalled campaign back on track? Answer: Execute a correct next event, one that addresses the problem condition and regains momentum.

Case Study

The process of automatically considering which one of four potential issues is a problem is extremely effective for qualifying and directing tactics, not only because the four directions define where an opportunity might be headed, but because it is a quick, accurate, response process. Once a salesperson ingrains the process, the process takes over, and the requirement to be creative, while under pressure, is drastically reduced

The very best case study of process deployment that comes to mind is not from the field of selling but from a Marine flight training school incident that occurred in 1987 in Orange County, California at the El Toro Marine Base.

The machine the young pilot was flying that day was an A-6 Fighter Jet, the precursor to today's F-A-18D Super Hornet. Awesome machines!

The training flight started with all systems ready, so the pilot fired the A-6 down the runway. As the plane lifted off, at a ground speed of about 129 knots, even though airborne, the A-6 suddenly lost power, with the potential for unspeakable consequences, the young pilot immediately released his dud-bombs onto the empty airfield, harming nothing and no one, while reducing the weight of the aircraft by several hundreds of pounds. Then, with the jet lighter, in spite of reduced power, he circled the field and made a perfect landing.

I read the account the following day in the newspaper and learned how close the pilot and perhaps the adjoining neighborhood had come to tragedy. The following day, I happened to see a friend of mine who was an officer at the base, and so naturally we talked about the near mishap. I told him how proud the Marines must be of that young pilot, how quickly and correctly he reacted, how superbly he averted disaster. My friend's response, "Yes, we are proud of him for how he performed. But you know, what he did was exactly what he was trained to do. He had been trained in a process that works when under pressure. The worst time to have to get creative is when you are under pressure."

When you are in the heat of a sales campaign battle, particularly when you are conducting a high-level meeting with key influencing people and decision-makers present, especially with hundreds of thousands of dollars at stake, that is pressure with a capital "P." That is when you need a process that works and one that doesn't test your creativity, as the officer said, "At the worst possible time." A standard process is a priceless skill to acquire. When you acquire this skill you no longer gamble your time or the resources of your organization.

Significant Point of Review

- The key to wearing well, long term, with a potential client is about being an exceptionally good listener and getting a good feel for identifying the reason why a campaign has slowed somewhat...credibility, value proposition, funding or timing.

- When all the previous events have been managed to your satisfaction, and closure is not happening as expected, the most suspect reason is the issue of timing. Caution... Never put pressure on your potential client at this point. Never attempt to re-sell your product. Instead, treat the decision maker the way you would want to be treated if you were in his shoes with a valid reason for delaying...and a reason that for the moment is proprietary.

- Practice the process. Remember, when pressure is at its highest point, it is the worst time to have to suddenly be creative. Ingrain the system described.

CHAPTER 10

Winning Campaigns Concurrently

Put another way, how do you win more than one big opportunity at a time? Account managers who conduct campaigns in a "one at a time" serial fashion are the first to go out of business. They are the first to be laid off during down times. The truth is this. Given enough time, enough resources, a superior product and a warm-hearted, understanding client, loaded with cash, most account managers can close a large opportunity once in a while. However, when those conditions are reversed, when the quarterly clock is running, when it takes more than one contract to hit target, being able to run concurrent campaigns separates the pros from the amateurs. The amateur's recipe for going out of business is very simple.

Here is an assessment of the typical account manager's habits during a typical quarter of chasing approximately six bigger opportunities:

- Six active opportunities at the beginning of the quarter
- Mid-quarter, four active opportunities in the funnel
- Mid-quarter, best opportunity gets 70% of the salesperson's focus
- Mid-quarter, second best gets 20% of the salesperson's focus
- Mid-quarter, third best opportunity gets 10% of the salesperson's focus
- Mid-quarter, number four opportunity gets zero focus from anybody. Call it the law of declining focus or whatever you like. The fact is that the scenario just outlined represents a serious problem for any organization that depends on the closure of significant, quarterly opportunities. You can be assured that what has just been described repeats itself every quarter of every year again and again and again. This quarterly pattern defines the "one at a time salesperson," and it is a perfect recipe for going out of business.

At the conclusion of the quarter, if the number one opportunity comes in, everyone breathes a sigh of relief! If both number one and number two find their way to the corporate corral, you can hear the corks popping in the next county! Nothing touches off celebrations like winning!

However, a mood bearing a striking resemblance to a funeral dirge sets in quickly when the potential client doesn't seem to know his part of the script and the opportunity everyone was counting on gets delayed or lost. At that moment account managers get serious counseling! Sales managers get equally serious counseling! And you can bet that if things don't get turned around in a hurry, even more serious discussions begin at the senior management level. Somebody always pays for losing! Harsh fact of life!

It has been said many times that a problem well-defined is already half-solved.

Just as there is a pattern for failure, there is a pattern for success in the pursuit of large Enterprise campaigns that require months of sales management. Fundamentally, managing more than one significant opportunity at a time involves two basic concepts and practices.

First, the salesperson and sales team must understand the event-driven flow of the sales campaign. That knowledge produces two huge benefits:

- Far-sighted anticipation of events equates to superior event execution. Proactive versus reactive event management wins every time in the execution effort. End of story!

Efficient process wins every time over lack of process, i.e., where the wheel gets recreated anew every time. Efficient processes that win produce the tremendous benefit of compacting big-ticket campaigns. Think of the value of being able to reduce your sales cycle by 30%, perhaps by half!

The second developed skill is being able to handle more than one significant opportunity at a time. Concurrent campaign management is practicing an organizational mindset based on the four substantive conditions discussed previously that must converge in order to conclude a successful campaign.

Significant Points of Review

- Conducting one-at-a-time campaigns is okay if you have a wide-base of clients producing adequate revenue.

- Without a solid base of average-size clients, learning to conduct multiple campaigns concurrently is an invaluable skill and will insure your long term success.

CHAPTER 11

FINAL THOUGHTS

The world is full of people who think they are doing you a favor by telling you what you can't do.

The world is full of managers who keep reminding you of areas where you need to improve your habits or skill set.

Couple of quick suggestions:

First, avoid relationships with those who are experts on what you should not try. Don't go near those who tell you that you can't.

Second, don't work for managers or companies who are more concerned with your weaknesses rather than your strengths.

Always…Always focus, instead, on leveraging you strengths. When you focus on your assets, you are in the best position to excel and win.

That does not mean that you can't develop new skills. This book is about developing the skill to win complex Enterprise campaigns. But in developing that skill, do be in a "can do" frame of mind.

Finally, the greatest coaches become great because they have, as part of their DNA, the gift of convincing people of what they can achieve. While in my dreams I would not put myself among those, encouraging is what I have tried to do in this book.

Significant Points of Review

- Always be focused on the positive and leveraging your personal strengths.
- Develop close relationships with those who believe in you and have your best interests at heart. Avoid the naysayers.

About the Author

I spent my career in sales and sales management with good companies: IBM, Tektronix, Mentor Graphics, Cadence Design Systems, etc.

After 25 years in the business of selling products and services, I began to focus narrowly on teaching and coaching sales teams on complex enterprise sales campaigns.

After retiring from corporate employment, I continued my coaching as an independent sales consultant. Companies retain me to coach account managers and support staff for important campaigns in process.

Recommendations

"My Major Accounts Team for Mentor Graphics was responsible for over $100M in Major Account business. Managing complex sales cycles with customers like Motorola, Texas Instruments, General Electric and General Motors required a disciplined approach to major account management. Bud Suse was instrumental in both the establishment and execution of a major accounts sales campaign methodology that successfully dissected, profiled and documented how to capture, maintain and grow our revenues in these large deal opportunities that involved very complex sales cycles.

Following my career with Mentor Graphics, I joined Gemstone Systems, where I have used many of the concepts that Bud created to build a global presence with major accounts such as Citicorp,

JP Morgan, Credit Suisse, UBS, Defense Intelligence Agency, Nokia and Siemans."

Dan Ware, Senior Executive Vice President, Gemstone Systems

Our company, again, retained Bud Suse to collaborate with our sales organization to capture specific, large sales opportunities

Together, Bud and I planned and executed an effective sales campaign strategy to win a very significant major account, one of the three largest companies of its industry in North America. At the beginning of the sales campaign, there were twelve competitors, and we were ranked next to last: but we decided to be the little engine that could. With the right mind-set and the right plan, and after a few months of meticulous campaign management, we moved into first place and won this award: a multi-million dollar, multi-year contract.

Clemens Spengler, Principle, The Spengler Group

"As a sales consultant, Bud Suse was instrumental in helping our organization win several large contracts in highly competitive situations. The structure of Bud's unique approach toward complex sales campaigns breaks down key components into manageable pieces. This system has made our entire sales group more productive by eliminating guesswork. Bud is a true sales professional and would be a valuable resource to any sales organization."

Dick O'Neil, a VP of Marketing

Authors note: I thank each person who has been so generous in these supporting comments. When I reflect on the joint effort we made to win significant campaigns, it is with deep appreciation I feel for them. I am grateful for their praise, and I would not go back and change a single thing.

On another point regarding the style of writing I use in this book...

Throughout this book, for simplicity's sake, and for ease of reading, I chose to use the pronoun "he," "him" and "his" instead of "she or he", "him or her," etc. I mean no disrespect to women and I trust that female readers will understand my intent.

Contact Information:

Bud Suse

Phone: 760-742-0205

760-500-2235

Email: nbsuse@gmail.com

Made in the USA
San Bernardino, CA
14 August 2019